RAINWATER HARVESTING MADE EASY

A BEGINNER'S GUIDE TO BUILD AND MAINTAIN YOUR OWN SUSTAINABLE CLEAN WATER SYSTEM FOR YOUR URBAN HOME, RURAL FARM, OR HOMESTEAD

PERENNIAL PUBLISHING

CONTENTS

INTRODUCTION

I enjoy the rain. I enjoy singing, dancing, bathing, and drinking it. Our bodies contain more than 70% water. Human beings are walking, talking rain!

The rain represents life. It replenishes the water in our aquifers, rivers, and springs. It keeps us cool, makes the land green, and nourishes the food-producing plants. It purifies the air, removes salts from the soil, and brings out the best in the animals.

However, the amount of fresh water on the planet is limited. The amount of fresh, readily available water on Earth is less than 2%. The remainder is frozen or saltwater. Rainfall is the only thing that replenishes our supply; it is a priceless gift from the heavens. So, we can't afford to waste it. Many people have grown so accustomed to being able to turn on the faucet and instantly have as much water as they want that they forget there is a limit. Only so much usable water exists on the planet, so we must use it wisely to best take care of ourselves, our communities, and the environment. You may be thinking, "But this problem is so big. What could I, one person, possibly do about it?" Well, my friend, mark this as the moment when that kind of thinking began to evolve.

I'm going to take you on a journey that will leave you excited and empowered to take action and change things for the better. Not only am I going to tell you stories of how ordinary people took that step of faith and used rainwater harvesting systems to completely change their lives and their entire community. I'm also going to walk you through the process so that you can learn how to do it yourself.

This book is my way of encouraging many others to try out a system that has greatly helped me and hundreds of others. In this book, you will learn how to build water harvesting systems that will allow rainwater to permeate and improve our landscapes, gardens, yards, parks, farms, and ranches. Home-scale tactics are the most efficient and affordable; hence they are highlighted in this guide. They are also the safest and most straightforward to complete. They can enable you to gain water independence.

Other than easing your water bills, there are tons of other benefits. With it, we can lessen erosion, flooding, water pollution, and mosquito breeding. We can use the rain that falls on your property to benefit your property even after the rainy season ends. The process also produces a remarkable variety of resources: It can produce high-quality irrigation water, drinking water, support vegetation that acts as living air conditioners and filters, reduce utility costs, improve soil fertility, grow food and beautify the area, expand the availability of local water resources, lessen the demand for groundwater, improve wildlife habitat, and give us and our neighborhood self-reliance and cooperation skills.

Anyone who wants to capture rainwater in a secure, beneficial, and sustainable manner should read this book. Whether you live in an urban or rural area, on a large or little piece of land, you may also be the expert and steward of your property. This book discusses water harvesting, including what it is, how to accomplish it, and how to use it for your specific site's characteristics. The goal is to achieve optimum effectiveness with the least amount of work and expense. Designing new water-harvesting landscapes or modifying existing ones will be the key point.

You will become a planner and designer and will learn how to create integrated settings and more effective plans suitable for both dryland towns and those with plenty of water. The creation and upkeep of water-harvesting earthworks will be discussed so that all landscapers and gardeners can also have something to take home. Activists will discover how water-harvesting initiatives can strengthen communities, foster a sense of place, and unite people.

Harvesting rainwater lessens the effects of dry weather, droughts, and floods. By maximizing rainwater capture, we can protect our fields from extreme weather conditions and climate change while increasing their resilience.

My objective is to help you see the value of rainfall and be able to start using it as your own water supply, either as your whole home system for all your water needs or to keep your landscaping looking vibrant in the dry season without needing to tap into municipal resources.

1

ALL THE ESSENTIAL INFO

"*For over 40 years, Zephaniah Phiri Maseko lived, farmed, and raised a family in one of the aridest and resource-poor lands in southern Africa, Zimbabwe's Zvishavane District. Through his ingenuity and despite political challenges, he devised and propagated irrigation practices that enabled subsistence farmers on marginal lands to prosper as they conserve scarce resources and practice sustainable farming.*

Phiri was born in 1927. As a young adult, he was jailed by the Rhodesian government for political activity, then released and blacklisted. Unable to obtain a paid job, he was ultimately forced to support his six children through full-time subsistence farming. Beginning in 1966 on a rocky and barren plot of land, he studied rainfall patterns and experimented with terraces and reservoirs, catchments and canals, infiltration pits, and fish ponds. His methods retained the scarce rainfall and raised the local water table. He won governmental praise in 1973 amid a severe drought and taught his methods to local farmers."

— *The Water Harvester* by Mary Kitoshynsky

The story above is just one of the success stories of how a dry wasteland could be turned into an oasis through rainwater harvesting. In fact, the inspiration gotten from this story which eventually led to the immense transformation of rainwater harvesting in Kenya cannot be overemphasized. So inspiring that Mr. Brad Lancaster, after paying a visit to Mr. Zaphaniah, had to write a book about the level of transformation that he saw 19 years later. Over the course of 30 years, a place that was formerly a wasteland has now been turned into an oasis by mere collection of rain. According to Lancaster, there was water everywhere and lots of vegetation. Some areas of the farm had thick vegetation for nesting birds that one had to call out loudly to be able to hear their own voice. Some parts contained abundant fruits, such as mangoes, that many of them even began to rot because the family and visitors couldn't keep up with the harvest. What was even more incredible was the attraction of wildlife to the farm due to the new vegetation growth. Many wild animals that were seldom seen in the area due to human activity began to roam in some parts. The latest animal visitor to be spotted were zebras! It was really incredible. Lancaster was so moved by what he saw that he couldn't contain his praises of how just by working in synergy with natural patterns could bring such wonderful results.

WHAT IS RAINWATER HARVESTING?

The purpose of rainwater harvesting is to collect and dispense rainwater for reuse on-site rather than letting it run off. The practice of rainwater harvesting varies greatly, from where rainwater is collected to how it is ultimately used.

A more accurate definition of rainwater harvesting is the process of collecting rainwater from a surface to store and use it later. Most rainwater harvesting systems collect rainwater from impervious surfaces, like roofs, and then store it in tanks or cisterns. There are other surfaces on which rainwater can be collected as well. Surfaces that permit easy collection of rainwater include driveways, roadways, and parking lots.

A wide variety of uses can be derived from rainwater, such as stormwater management, potable and non-potable for indoor use, and landscape irrigation. In situations where no other water source is available or where the available water supply is inadequate or of poor quality, harvested rainwater can be particularly useful.

Rainwater harvesting, abbreviated as RWH, is beneficial for both urban and rural properties. There are a variety of ways to harvest and utilize rainwater, such as using rain barrels under gutter downspouts or supplying a home with potable water using systems that supply the water for the house.

ORIGINS OF RAINWATER HARVESTING

Growing up, my grandfather talked about the old rain cistern on his farm. Water would be stored in these cisterns for cattle and other livestock so that they drink from them to cool off during a hot day.

During rainy seasons, rainwater would be delivered into the cisterns using gutters and conveyances. Although this is another step in the evolution of rainwater harvesting, it's still a long way from where it all began.

Even though it is almost impossible to pinpoint which civilization used RWH first, the evidence available shows that India, Mesopotamia, China, and the area that is today called Israel all used different types of rainwater collection systems in 2000 BC.

Middle East

Historically, RWH has been a significant part of the Middle East. Water from the hillside was collected and stored in cisterns in the Negev Desert, which is in modern-day Israel, as far back as 2000 B.C.

It was a true life-or-death situation back then when water was hard to come by. In *Design for Water,* Heather Kinkade-Levario explains that king Mesha of Moab captured rain in reservoirs and provided his warriors with the ability to survive in the dry heat during the war for the land east of Jordan.

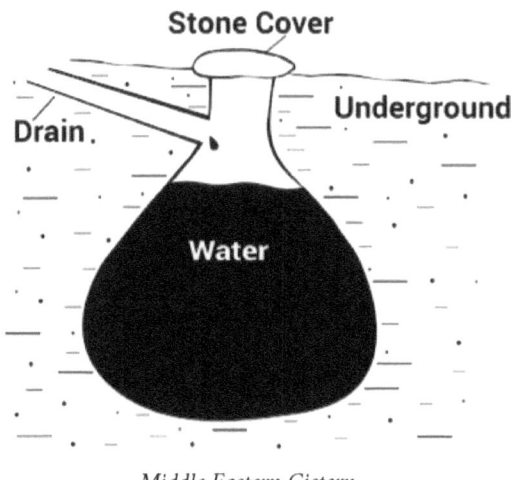

Middle Eastern Cistern

Based on historical documents from that time in the Middle East, RWH cisterns were common in that civilization. In many cases, these cisterns were underground, with a capacity of 10,000 gallons to 50,000 gallons. There were also many community cisterns. Water could be stored in a large cistern that can hold 1,000,000 gallons using technology such as sediment traps. Even larger reservoirs, such as the one in Madaba, Jordan, can hold 11,000,000 gallons of water.

India

Farmers in Kutch, India, and Balochistan (now Iran, Pakistan and Afghanistan) used rainwater harvesting for agriculture and many other uses around 300 BC. The Chola Kings harvested rainwater as well. A rainwater collection tank called the Shivaganga tank collected rainwater at the Brihadeeswarar temple (located in Balaganpathy Nagar, Thanjavur, India). Another tank, the Vīrānam tank, was built in the Cuddalore district of Tamil Nadu in the later Chola period (1011 to 1037 AD) to store drinking and irrigation water. Vīrānam is a 10-mile-long (16 km) storage tank containing 11 billion gallons (41,500,000 cubic meters) of storage.

India still has infrastructure and evidence of RWH, such as Talibs, medium-sized reservoirs that are used for irrigation and drinking; Johads, dams which capture and hold rainwater; baoris, wells dug into the ground to provide drinking water; and Jhalaras, tanks designed specifically for the local community and religious purposes.

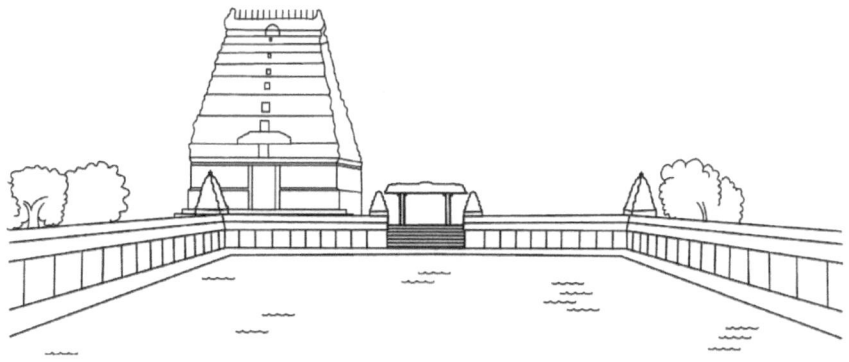

Indian Shivaganga Tank

Ancient Rome

There were many technological advancements made by the Romans, including harvesting rainwater and building aqueducts. It was common for entire cities to be built with the infrastructure for diverting rainwater into large cisterns. The water was used by the Romans for drinking, washing, bathing, irrigation, and livestock.

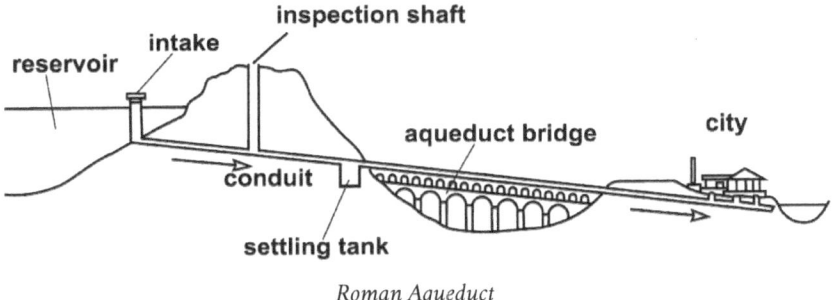

Roman Aqueduct

They were master engineers. In fact, there is a rainwater collection cistern built to capture rainwater from the streets above in the Sunken Palace, Istanbul that remains to this day, and it is so large that you can sail in it.

Mayans

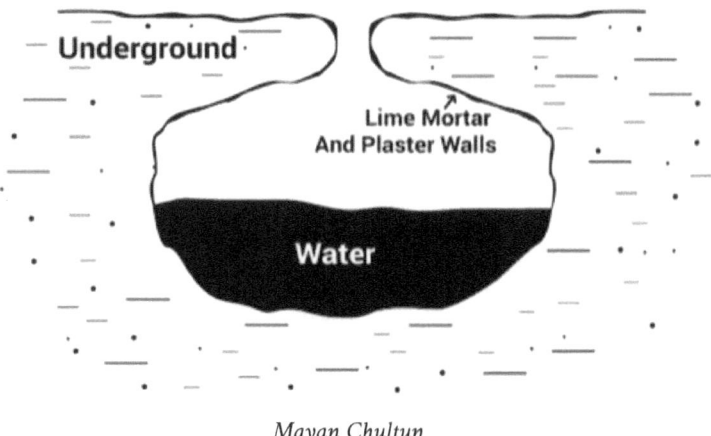

Mayan Chultun

The region of the Yucatan Peninsula, inhabited by the Mayans, thrived on an intelligently built civilization, sound technologies, and strong educational systems with advanced knowledge in astronomy and mathematics. This popular pre-Columbian civilization is famous for outstanding architecture, monuments, and, most importantly, a well-engineered water storage system that sustained the Mayans even amid a drought. Their ingenuity spurred on the creation of a complex organization of cisterns described as chultuns, which involved altering their landscape to harvest and store available rainwater.

During the rainy season, the Mayans depended on sacred water-filled caves as their useful water source. Once these caves dried out, they began creating cisterns (chultuns) curated as an underground rainwater storage chamber and coated them with lime mortar and plaster to prevent stored water from leaking. The constant and heavy use of lime mortar and plaster had quite a negative impact on their environment, raising a major deforestation challenge because about twenty trees would have to be burnt to create a useful amount of lime plaster. They further created unique connections responsible for circulating water in cities even in dry seasons.

However, it was quite unfortunate that the Mayans' great technological advancement and classic civilization, especially in complex water storage, began to collapse around the 8th and 9th centuries. Speculations as regards the cause of this fall include environmental depreciation, natural disasters, wars, or a summation of all speculations.

North America

The terms 'hard water' and 'soft water' originated in North America between the 16th and 17th centuries. This term was in constant use when ancient Native Americans noticed the disparity between mineral-rich water and rainwater when washing their clothes. They realized that using hard, mineral-rich water causes the unpleasant formation of buildup when used with soap, while soft water reacts minimally with soap and washes off dirt quickly and thoroughly.

Ancient North America was prone to drought. As a result, settlers from the southwestern region's Pueblo, Hopi, Mojave, and Bavojo tribes created dances linked to spiritual practices and belief in rainmaking gods. These dances were performed in specific seasons, especially when drought was near and unfavorable weather conditions threatened crops. Settlers also survived by taking advantage of mountains to collect rainwater via gravity and directing this harvested rainwater to a network of underground cisterns.

Decline in Use

The swift advancement of modern civilization and technologies has discouraged using ancient rainwater harvesting systems. As of now, only your grandma or grandpa might be able to provide you with full and vivid details of how this process of harvesting rainwater works. Also, specific reasons such as the extensive use of water pipes and reservoirs, recurring incidence of cistern contamination, and a rise in cases of diseases and infections contributed to the decline in the rainwater harvesting system.

Modern water pipes can easily be recognized and have been designed to transport clean and treated water easily from reservoirs to areas where it is needed. These reservoirs are durable and easily installed within your space; an example of such a durable reservoir is water storage tanks made with polyethylene, steel, or fiberglass. Some reservoirs are huge and created for a large population or agricultural activities; a typical example of such a reservoir is a dam. The emergence of these modern water storage systems has pushed ancient water harvesting and storage methods into the book of archaic practices and created a more centralized means of unlimited water supply.

The success rates associated with the historic system of rainwater harvesting using underground cisterns were very high and encouraged the rapid growth of civilizations. The emergence of a quickly growing populations increased the dependence on these cisterns to be able to satisfy household and agricultural needs. As a result of this pressure, cisterns became challenged with the issue of contamination, and unfortunately, diseases began to spread faster than available technologies could curb the spread. When countries began a new development phase, new technologies and measures were implemented to create a system where they could more easily prevent the spread of disease with the knowledge they had. Does this mean rainwater harvesting is an outdated practice that should stay in the past? Definitely not. It's actually making a quite a comeback. We know more about how disease works and how to prevent it than we did back then. By using proper sanitation practices that we now have a much better understanding of, you can safely use, even safely drink, harvested rainwater. As we go through this book, you'll get to hear more stories of people who have successfully implemented rainwater harvesting in more modern times.

ADVANTAGES AND DISADVANTAGES OF RAINWATER HARVESTING TODAY

+ *Advantages*

1. Saves money

I appreciate innovations that can help me save money, and I believe you do too. Gifts are free, and rainwater is one gift that falls on your roof for free. The process of rainwater harvesting can be very cheap. Water companies charge high prices due to the high cost of construction of dams, bore-holes, treatment tanks, and pipes, coupled with the expense of maintaining these laid down structures. Don't forget you can also meet your garden and agricultural needs at a very cheap price.

2. Decrease water demand

Harvested rainwater decreases dependence on the usual neighborhood or city's water supply. In cases where you have to use heavy volumes of water to cater to the water needs of your large household, the simple functionality of your rainwater storage system lets you bypass the normal water supply. You get to experience the satisfaction of achieving self-reliance for basic household needs like wash-ing, drinking, bathing, and cooking.

3. Promotes water and energy conservation

Treating and pumping water from dams or water plants requires a huge amount of energy to maintain the right amount of pressure and temperature and to transport clean water to consumers at a fast pace. Harvesting rainwater helps to minimize the amount of energy consumed by this modern water supply system and minimize the risk of environmental pollution.

4. Improves quality and quantity of groundwater

Adopting the principle of rainwater harvesting and encouraging commercial use of rainwater helps save water accumulated underground as groundwater. It is also important to note that the resulting advantage is that clean water would be readily available for important uses while using harvested rainwater for emergency purposes such as a fire outbreak.

5. No treatment system is needed for landscape irrigation

Rainwater harvested with simple filters to keep out debris such as leaves and sticks does not need to be thoroughly treated at the microscopic level to be beneficial for agricultural landscape irrigation. As long as you keep up with routine maintenance, including keeping your storage container clean, you can easily make water available for your farming needs without worrying about negative effects of this harvested water on your plants.

6. Relatively simple

Creating a basic rainwater harvesting system is an easy process. All you need is a catchment area, such as your roof, where the rainfall flows to your simple filtering system to eliminate debris in storage tanks. If you want something more sophisticated, you can absolutely do that. But a system doesn't have to be complicated to be useful.

7. Reduces environmental pollution and contamination

Rainwater that fails to be absorbed by the earth ends up as runoff and can pose a great environmental risk. These risks include soil degradation or erosion, flooding, and trans-portation of harmful chemicals, fertilizers, metals, pesticides, and other contaminants into the water. Diligent collection of rainwater can help minimize these risks' emergence and prevalence.

— *Disadvantages*

1. Unpredictable rainfall

It's joked that the easiest job in the world is a meteorologist because even if your forecast is wrong every single day, you still have a job. No one is surprised when you predict the wrong weather.

It's hard to know exactly how much rain you'll get and when you'll get it. Because of this between rainstorms you could run out of stored rainwater if you don't have enough storage space.

2. High cost for large-scale, entire homestead setup

Rainwater harvesting systems can vary widely in complexity. Storing rainwater, for example, just to irrigate your backyard garden can be quite cheap. However, if you want a sophisticated, high-volume system that will provide water for your whole home and extensive farm, it can get pretty pricey. This is especially true if you want to create new earthworks, such as dig a cistern or build swales with commercial equipment. If you dream of complete water independence, my advice to you is to start small. Make a plan for what you want your system to eventually look like and implement it one step at a time. It won't all come together overnight, but if you commit to accomplishing one part at a time, you will eventually have the system you've always wanted.

3. Requires maintenance

Once you've created your rainwater harvesting system, the next challenge is to constantly keep it under strict maintenance to avoid insects, rodents, mosquitoes, algae, and lizard infestation. You'll need to take time to clean the environment surrounding this storage system regularly. Check for leaks, broken seals, and other technical difficulties that might arise.

4. Storage limits

Rainwater harvesting is fun, especially in the rainy season, until there is a heavy downpour and your storage system cannot hold any more water. It can be disappointing to know that you could have had more water saved for the dry season, but instead, it ran off your property. A solution to this is, when time, space, and money permit, to connect an additional storage tank to your current one. You can upgrade to a larger container if you like, but as long as the original one is still in good shape, there is no need to throw it away. Connect the two and you can use both to store as much water as possible.

5. Chemical and animal dropping

It will interest you—or disgust you—to know that your roof probably contains droppings from birds, rodents, and remains of insects. Some roofs also contain harmful corrosive chemicals, such as those made with asbestos or lead roofing. All these contaminants can easily flow along with the rainwater you're trying to harvest, thereby posing serious harm to your farmland if they aren't filtered out. It would be wise to check what kind of shingles your roof was made with before installing your system.

6. Complete water independence is not easy

The basic and most important household need for water is drinking. Rainwater, when it is first harvested, is not fit for drinking. It will have to undergo several filtration processes before it can become fit for complete household and agricultural use. Another downside is that local authorities might decide to regulate your rainwater harvesting system once you've put everything in place to make it your primary source of water supply.

Harvesting rainwater is fun and highly rewarding regardless of the disadvantages surrounding it. The good news about those disadvantages is that they are surmountable, and the advantages of harvesting rainwater outweigh the negative side of this highly beneficial system of storing water for long-term use.

Many conservationists and environmental experts believe that we haven't reached the peak of rainwater harvesting. With the rise and complexities in technologies and civilization, rainwater harvesting is becoming popular, easier, and more beneficial every day.

2

USES OF HARVESTED RAINWATER

MORE THAN JUST RAINWATER

In one of India's most terribly drought-prone regions lies the Hiware Bazar Village, now recognized as the "miracle water village." This village has a large population, including a farmer who battled with the ongoing negative effects of drought on his fifteen-acre farmland. Farming was taxing, yields were poor, and returns on investment were next to nothing. About twenty years ago, this farmer liaised with a group of other farmers to create a special rainwater harvesting system. This new system turned an impoverished village into an oasis blooming with great harvest, sound structures, booming civilization, and became the home of millionaire farmers. This story of Hiware Bazar's breakthrough is not just inspiring but a huge proof that the massive benefits of harvesting rainwater cannot be underestimated.

WILL HARVESTED RAINWATER CONTAMINATE MY CROPS?

Rainwater harvested from your roof is not totally clean. If you live in an urban area, there is a high chance of finding contaminants ranging from bird droppings, pollution from the exhaust of cars and factories, and most commonly, the remains of insects. When harvesting rainwater, it is important to treat the water properly using a filtration system as it's collected into your storage tanks.

The formation of algae in stored water poses serious risks to your crops because it competes with your plants for both nutrients and sunlight, making it difficult for your crop to reach maturity. You can solve this problem by using storage tanks that are not made with white or translucent material, as these types of tanks permit the penetration of sun rays into your harvested water. Remember that sunlight encourages the growth of algae.

Rainwater, when filtered and stored in a properly maintained storage tank, will not harm your edible crops. Take time to check for leaks and possible openings as they can become breeding points for mosquitoes, and several small animals might fall into the storage tank. Also, watch out for foul smells, and dispose of the water once you perceive it might be contaminated. Using contaminated rainwater on plants can cause stunting, discoloration, and even the death of plants.

APPLICATIONS

The application of harvested rainwater is quite diverse. You can use rainwater for household, commercial, and agricultural purposes. Try not to give room for panic but rest assured that once you follow the necessary procedures to ensure a perfectly clean rainwater storage system, you can proudly use your rainwater for basically anything, including drinking, laundry, flushing toilets, bathing, cooking, irrigation, farming, and grooming your beautiful flower garden. As I stated in the previous chapter, your harvested rainwater gives you the chance to save money, rely less on the general water supply, save you from the stress of sorting out bills, help you conserve energy, and give you the privilege of doing more for less.

If you live in an environment with a high incidence of wildfire, the process of harvesting rainwater will save you from an aggravated disaster once a fire outbreak arises. If you live far from a fire station, your steady source of water supply will come to your rescue.

INDOOR GENERAL PURPOSES AND POTABLE WATER

The purposes for which harvested rainwater serves you and your household cannot be overemphasized. Any water to be recognized as being potable must be completely fit for drinking. Harvested rainwater will satisfy potable water conditions once it has undergone thorough filtration and treatment. Potable water can be used for other household purposes aside from drinking. These purposes include; cooking, washing, and bathing.

Potable Uses of Rainwater

I. Cooking and Drinking

A lot of people question the use of rainwater for cooking, and my reply to them is that once your harvested rainwater has been thoroughly filtered and purified either with the use of chlorine sediments, or a mechanically powered cleaner, you can rest assured that your water is safe for cooking and drinking.

II. Washing and Cleaning

The household chore of washing and cleaning increases dependence and pressure on the commercial water supply. You can save yourself from the stress of worrying about the rising bills resulting from this dependence by making adequate use of your harvested rainwater.

Before using rainwater for your laundry, you must filter your water and ensure it's free from all forms of pollen or sediments. Also, purify your water using the correct amount of chlorine or by adopting the reverse osmosis method, which works by eliminating any form of impurity using a semi-permeable membrane.

III. Bathing

After thoroughly following the rainwater treatment procedure, you're free to use your harvested rainwater to shower yourself and your pets. You can also boil the water to enjoy efficient warmth.

IV. Watering Wildlife, Pets, and Livestock

If you have a pet, farm animals, or are a wildlife conservationist; you can be assured that you will reap the best of rainwater benefits on behalf of these animals. By connecting a pump to your water storage tank, you can send clean water directly to their troughs.

Non-potable Uses of Rainwater

I. Composting

The process of making compost requires the use of lots of water to speed up the rate at which organic waste decomposes. You can provide an adequate water supply using your harvested rainwater and aid the growth of healthy crops and a well-tailored garden.

II. Fire Prevention and Protection

If you live where there are reoccurring cases of fire, you can save yourself from unnecessary panic, stress, and danger by taking advantage of any rainwater that falls on your roof. Ensure that you collect rainwater in a large storage tank and make sure it is readily accessible whenever you need it.

III. Water Features/Ponds

Harvested rainwater can be useful in filling ponds and aesthetically pleasing water features. I will advise you to filter your rainwater to avoid clogging pumps or pipes. Also, clean the rainwater-filled ponds and water features to avoid the buildup of algae and discourage mosquitoes from turning it into a breeding ground. You can manipulate your ponds to be suitable for aquaculture.

IV. Rain gardens

Another useful purpose of rainwater is the aesthetic creation of plants that can adapt to water. You can source a range of plants that thrive in wet environments. Your harvested rain-water can be a good water source for your blooming water garden.

V. Flushing Toilets

One of the household's major concerns regarding water consumption is the quantity of water used to flush toilets every day. Taking advantage of rainwater for flushing your toilets helps you save clean water from your regular water reservoir and conserve energy because you don't have to spend so much time, energy, and resources on treating rainwater before use.

If you want to use non-potable rainwater in your home for flushing, you'll need to make sure to keep this water supply separate from your other household potable water. To have an efficient water supply for your toilet cisterns, you must create a separate simple flushing system. This system involves a network of pumps that carry water from ground level to a header tank which will propel water on pressure to the toilet cisterns.

IRRIGATION

Calculating How Much Water You Can Harvest

Before you begin to establish a stable irrigation system, I will advise you to figure out a rough estimate of possible expenses using an easy equation that will give you an idea of the total number of gallons of rainwater you can harvest from your roof. This equation is $S \times R \times 0.6$, where S is the size of your roof in square feet and R is the total amount of rainfall annually in inches. For example, if your house measures 10 feet by 20 feet, and the average annual rainfall in your region is about 20 inches, the number of gallons you can fill with harvested rainwater each year will be $(10 \times 20) \times 20 \times 0.6 = 2,400$ gallons of water. You don't need to consider the angle or slope of your roof in your calculation. Rain generally falls straight down, so you would collect the same amount if your roof was angled or flat. If you are not familiar with doing manual calculations, you can use online calculators to find this number for you.

Sizing the System

Your well-drafted budget and the amount of space available will determine the size of your rainwater harvesting system. A big budget and large expanse of land mean a big rainwater catchment, while a small budget and land mean you will have to prepare for a small rainwater harvesting system. Rainwater from your catchment is kept in storage tanks made up of several materials that you are free to pick from based on aesthetic needs, price, and quality. The most common storage tank is the plastic or polyethylene tank, which can be bought at a farm supply or online store.

I usually advise people who have little space, but want to have the biggest system possible to opt for two or three portable and durable tanks that can store up to fifty gallons of water instead of going for larger tanks which can be inconvenient when you want to get them installed. Smaller tanks are easy to move around and give your landscape a nice look without taking up too much space.

Connecting to the Irrigation System

Your irrigation system does not have to be complex. It can be as straightforward as connecting a pipe to the spigot at the bottom of the rainwater storage tank. This way, gravity does the work for you. It will work best if the elevation of your garden or farmland is lower than that of the water level in the storage tank.

It may not be feasible on your property to simply let gravity direct the flow of water; perhaps the space you want to irrigate is large enough that water will need extra coaxing to get where you need it to be. You'll want to add a water pump to your system. A wide range of conduits, such as valves, pumps, and pump accessories, deliver an accurate amount of pressure to your irrigation system when transporting water from your storage tank. The advancement of technology has led to the creation of automated irrigation systems, which have certain valves and controls that work according to how it has been programmed. Make sure you use a filter with fine quality of about three to five macron to avoid clogging irrigation systems. Doing this will increase the life span of your pumps and irrigation emitter. Once you delve into including pumps in your water harvesting system, it can get quite a bit more complicated. But areas of opportunity where you can now use the rainwater on your land open up, which is really exciting.

STORAGE TANKS

Your irrigation system requires a storage tank that meets the specifications of your needs and available space. When searching for suitable tanks, several factors come into play, such as the amount of rainfall you get in your area, the amount of money at hand, your water demand during dry seasons, the irrigation area, and your aesthetics.

Based on my experience, here is a list of recommendations when shopping for a storage tank.

I. Ensure that the tank was made with quality materials from such as polyethylene, corrugated steel, or fiberglass.

II. Avoid buying storage tanks that are translucent or made of white material because they can encourage the passage of sunlight into your preserved rainwater and lead to the formation of algae. I do not appreciate the presence of algae in my irrigation system because it can ruin the growth and maturity of plants.

III. Ensure that the tank is well covered with its vents properly screened, so you don't go home to a tank infested with insects, lizards, or frogs.

IV. Plan for your storage tank to be located close to the area you want to irrigate. The last thing you want is for the overflow outlet to flow directly to your house or septic pits. This can damage your home's foundation or spread sewage across your yard. Neither of those are problems I want anyone to have to deal with.

V. If you are sure you have chosen the best place for your tanks and you will not want to move them in the future, you can opt for storage tanks that can contain two hundred to three hundred gallons of harvested rainwater. They can be purchased in several numbers depending on the area you wish to irrigate. Tanks like these are commercially available, with overflow ports to link one barrel to the other.

IMPACTS OF ROOFING MATERIALS ON RAINWATER HARVESTING

Apart from the animal droppings, remains of insects, and chemical pollutants from the atmosphere, the material from which your roof is made can positively or negatively impact your harvested rainwater. The good news is that most roofing materials are safe for this purpose. Asphalt shingles, which are the most common roofing material, are safe for rainwater harvesting. The only thing to keep in mind with this is that although the shingles are safe, the adhesive used to install the shingles may not be as safe. When this roofing material is first installed, the adhesive begins an off-gassing process which will leach into the water. After a year, most of this process is done, and at the three-year mark, it will be effectively finished. Less common but still a safe catchment area are Galvalume (a zinc and aluminum alloy with a non-toxic coating), powder coated or enameled, and standing seam roofs.

Corrugated metal is normally safe, but occasionally people have issues with zinc from these roofs leaching into their water. If zinc levels are too high, it will make the water unsafe to drink and harmful to your plants. Wood shingles are also in this maybe ok, maybe not category. The wood is nearly always treated, which could introduce chemicals that are not safe for drinking. However, this water is normally suitable for watering your garden. A good way to get an idea of if your roofing will cause problems for your veggies is to take a look at the grass around your downspout. Is the water currently coming off of your roof damaging your grass? If not, great! If it is, you will need to either choose a different catchment area or test your water and treat it according to your test findings.

There are many other roofing materials that are not as common but are also safe for rainwater harvesting. If it's not in the following list of roofing materials that are not good for rainwater harvesting, you're probably fine. But I do recommend testing the water that comes out of your down-spout before installing your system. This way, no matter what your roof is made of, you can be 100% sure it is safe, and if there are any concerns, you can plan ahead to have the necessary treatments and filters to combat anything unwanted in your new water supply.

Though most roofing materials are good for our purposes, there are a few I would caution you against. Lead, asbestos, and copper roofing can cause problems. Lead is not very common but is potentially dangerous enough to your health that I at least recommend testing to be sure you don't ingest it. Asbestos roofing became popular in the 1900s due to being much sturdier than the previously used slate shingle, with the added benefit of being fireproof. The public became aware of the health hazards of asbestos in the late 1900s, and it was quickly banned. Copper roofing is favored by some because of its ability to inhibit algae and moss growth, which can be a problem, especially in the Pacific Northwest. That is because copper, as well as zinc, are herbicides. While that is useful for keeping a moss-prone roof cleaner, it's not good for our gardens. Also, be cautious of copper or zinc coated shingles for the same reason.

Rainwater harvesting systems are very versatile. They are so many potential uses and ways to make them that you get to customize it all to what will work best for you. With that in mind, how do you want to use your harvested rainwater?

3

PRINCIPLES AND COMPONENTS

In 2016, the history of the drought-plagued Kolila Joga was written by vibrant youths who took it upon themselves to change their entire village's future. These young and able-bodied men dug the ground restlessly for days with simple hoes and shovels to turn a small pond into a major rainwater catchment system. Before the emergence of those youths, Kolija Joga, situated in Rajasthan two years before the breakthrough, was solely dependent on the scarce water supply provided by the government for household and agricultural purposes.

When the breakthrough story began, efforts made by these youths were noticed, and the officials decided to broaden the project, making it a state scheme for the process of rainwater harvesting. Soon enough, excavators and earth movers were deployed to the area. Not too long after, the small pond became an unbelievable twenty-six-hectare rainwater harvesting area with an outstanding capacity of seven thousand, six hundred and thirty cubic meters. This capacity was duly confirmed by the superintendent engineer of the Rajasthan watershed department, Hiralal Singh.

This success story made Kalila Joga one of the very first villages to partake in the state's water conservation project. Since its inception in 2016, seven thousand, seven hundred and forty villages have been blessed with a steady water supply. Farming yields increased in multiple folds, getting water stopped being a tiring chore, and families were able to access clean drinking water. The story of Kolila Joga is strong motivation to take up the project of harvesting rainwater and amassing its benefits. Your willingness and desire alone are potent enough to make a difference regardless of the number of people available to support you.

THE PRINCIPLES OF RAINWATER HARVESTING

1. Start with thoughtful, careful, and long observation

Before you start the process of rainwater harvesting, you need to think carefully and observe your environment thoughtfully. Check out your watershed and study where the rainwater and its sediments flow. Draw a reasonable conclusion on what would work in your favor. Start your rainwater harvesting project at the highest point of your watershed, and then prepare for the next step.

2. Begin at the top (high-point) of your catchment and work your way down

The easiest point to collect your rainwater is at the top. This is because the water travels downward with less volume, a decrease in pressure, and lower water velocity. Collecting rainwater from a high point ensures unhindered penetration and an efficient distribution powered by gravity.

3. Start small and simple

You do not need to break your limits when trying to establish a rainwater harvesting system. Work according to your strength, capacity, knowledge, and resources. The smallest strategies that get accomplished are far better than the complicated ones that never even start.

4. Direct the movement of water

Manipulate the flow of rainwater for your catchment by encouraging the water to gather in a place, and penetrate the soil. This way, the water will not erode or degrade the land's surface.

5. Always plan an overflow pathway and regulate that overflow as a resource

Sometimes you might have more rain than you need; this rain may come as storms, which will cause floods and overflows. To effectively manage this problem, create a stable overflow route to divert heavy rain floods from eroding your land.

6. Maximize living and organic groundcover

Create an organic ground cover. This acts as a living sponge made up of specific plants that break down microorganisms and encourage water penetration into the soil, thereby improving the growth and maturity of plants.

7. Take full advantage of beneficial relationships and functionality by "stacking functions"

Do much more with your harvested rainwater by expanding your horizon or the extent to which you can use your harvested rainwater. You can strategically site several plants near the building with your rainwater harvesting system. The water is easily accessible to keep the plants happy while the plants are able to keep the building cool during the hot summer. You can also select specific vegetation that will provide food from time to time.

8. Reassess and examine your system, the "feedback loop," regularly

Try not to limit yourself to the previous principle, but continue to reapply all the principles I have explained as an important cycle. You are also free to explore and make innovations when needed.

These principles are the foundation of establishing a highly successful rainwater harvesting system. You must apply all principles to take full advantage of your site's potential, eliminate and avoid unnecessary errors, save costs, and achieve more than you can imagine without stress. The type of land-scape you have does not affect or change the principles listed above.

DIFFERENT COMPONENTS

Various components make up a rainwater harvesting system. These components vary in complexity and personal prefer-ences, including the process of receiving, channeling, trans-porting, purifying rainwater, and recharging the rainwater harvesting system.

The components of Rainwater Harvesting Systems are outlined below:

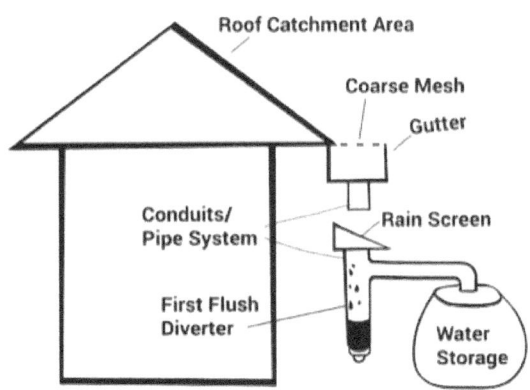

Rainwater Harvesting System Components

1. Catchment Area

This specific surface area is dedicated to receiving rainfall directly without hindrance. Your catchment area could be the roof of your house or shed, a paved lawn, or an open field. The vast majority of systems use a roof as the catchment area.

2. Gutters

When building a house, it's standard practice to install gutters below the roof. So, this is one component you probably already have. However, if you were planning on using the roof of a shed or other outbuilding as a catchment area, you'll need to install gutters. You can use the typical aluminum gutters that you see on most houses, or you can even get creative and do something different such as using PVC or bamboo. The size of the gutters should suit the average amount of rainfall your area gets annually. Ensure you fix and support gutters properly so they do not sag or collapse when overloaded with water.

3. Coarse Mesh

Anyone who has spent time cleaning out their gutters will easily agree with this one. Direct rain from the sky is pure, but unfortunately, the surface of your roof is not. Rain will direct dead insects and bird droppings from your roof into your gutters. Not only that, but if your house is next to trees, all of those beautiful fall leaves come down when the season changes and, unfortunately, land on your roof and end up in your gutters when it rains. This can be a huge pain to constantly dig piles of debris out of your gutters, so do yourself a favor. Install a mesh covering on your gutters.

4. Conduits or Piping Systems

First, the rain falls on your roof. Then it lands in your gutters. From your gutters, it needs a way to get to your storage tank. The conduits, also called the piping system, are what accomplish this task. Most commonly, this piping system is made with PVC.

5. First Flush Diverter

The first flush device is a one-way valve that works by flushing out the first spell of rain from your catchment area. It diverts water polluted with debris, animal droppings, insect remains, and dried leaves away from your rainwater harvesting system. The first flush system might not eliminate all contaminants, but it is an effective process. Though it may seem innocuous, whether to use a first flush diverter or not is actually a hotly disputed topic. I'll explain why in another chapter, but for now just know that this component is up to your discretion to use or not.

6. Rain Screen

Gutter mesh can't always catch everything, so a rain screen acts as a good backup. It is located under the downspout and positioned at a 45-degree position, which allows for easy sliding off of debris. The edges of rain screens are slightly raised to prevent water from overpouring, and the mesh covering is tiny enough to keep out debris and insects. More intricate systems usually have a rain screen, but if you want to keep it as simple as possible to start, you can forego this component for now.

7. Storage

These are structures that are designed to store your rainwater until you are ready to use it. Storage tanks can be made of various materials such as corrugated steel, polyethylene, concrete, or fiberglass. Make sure your tank is positioned level on the ground or underground, depending on your preference. When choosing a location for your tanks, make sure to keep in mind that they require diligent maintenance and cleaning so that you can use them for a long time.

8. Recharge Structures

When rainwater flows off of your property, you miss out on the opportunity for that water to replenish the groundwater underneath you. Recharge structures encourage rainwater to increase groundwater quantity by recharging the permeable rocks underground. These porous rocks are also known as aquifers. Aquifers can be recharged with a recharging structure through wells, trenches, or recharge pits.

Several recharging structures exist, which makes it possible for water to seep through the soil surface or transport water to higher soil depths where it merges with groundwater. One good thing about this component is that existing structures like pits, tanks, and wells can be turned into recharge structures, thereby saving you the stress of creating a new structure. There are several cheap and accessible recharge methods you can choose from.

I. Dug wells and tube wells

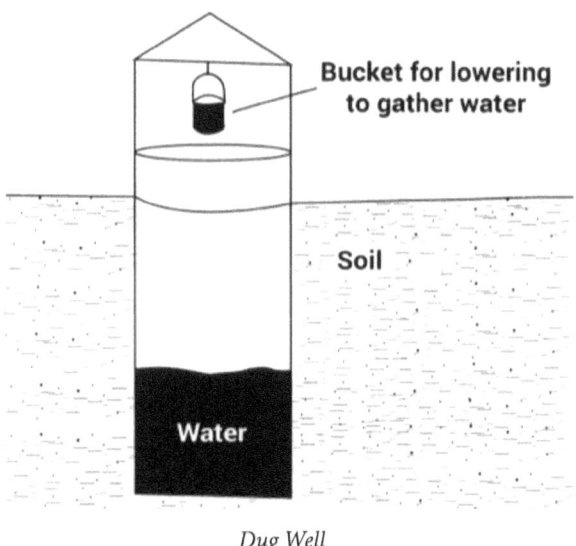

Dug Well

In areas filled with sands or landscapes created by running water and rocky areas, you can find innumerable quantities of wells that have dried up or with drastically reduced water levels. These wells can be recharged by collecting rainwater from a rooftop and directing this water via conduits to a filtration system, which then goes to refill your well.

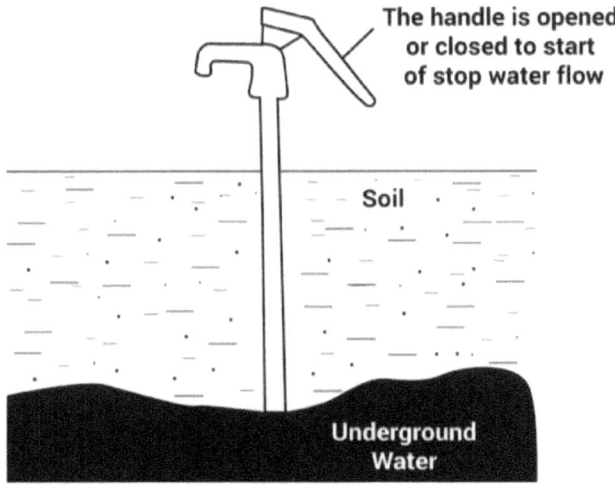

Tube Well

This can be done to tube wells or dug wells. Also, ensure you have your dug wells covered to discourage mosquitoes from converting them into a breeding ground and prevent the entry of contaminants. To ensure that you have quality rain-water entering your wells, fix a filtration system on your catchment area.

II. Injection wells

While dug wells and tube wells are initially made for the purpose of getting water out of the ground, injection wells are dug specifically to put water back in the ground.

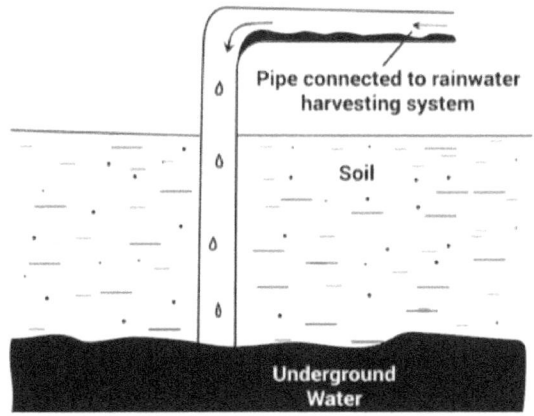

Injection Well

If you are looking for a way to recharge your groundwater but do not already have any wells, this is a good option for you. These look similar to tube wells, except there is no mechanism for getting water out of the ground, only pipes to direct water into the ground. Though not our purpose for digging an injection well, it's worth noting that not all injection wells are for recharging groundwater. There are also injection wells that are dug much further into the ground that are used to dispose of wastewater or industrial waste.

III. Recharge pits and trenches

This kind of recharge structure is another good option if you don't have a dry well already available to be converted to a recharge structure. Plus, this has the added benefit of being less technically complicated to make. These are made by digging a hole in the ground and filling it with layers of material. At the bottom will be large rocks. On top of that, smaller rocks, then sand, a layer of soil, and grass is planted on top. A recharge trench is made the same way, except rather than digging one large pit, a long narrow channel is dug.

These layers are beneficial in multiple ways. First, they act as a filter, so you will be recharging your groundwater with clean water. Also, the materials in these layers create an environment that makes it easy for water to flow downward.

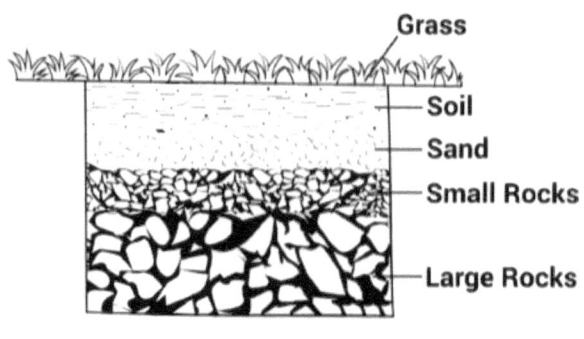

Recharge Pit

Deep layers of soil can become compacted or may contain high amounts of clay, which discourage the water from penetrating the ground enough to refill aquifers. By creating areas where it is easier for water to go down further into the ground, you increase groundwater as well as lower the amount of runoff from your land.

Another great thing that I like about these is that once they have been made, they can completely blend in with your landscaping. Since the top of a recharge pit or trench is covered with soil and vegetation, you can choose to plant whatever will match the surroundings. Once a year, these should be checked to see if any settling has occurred and if they need to have any material added.

What are Earthworks?

Earthworks are special constructions made with lots of earth (soil). Examples include berms, levees, canals, railway beds, and dams. It is an engineering process of removing, refilling, and remolding soil matter and converting it into useful structures. We will be focusing on the ones that are created to reduce dependence on irrigation.

Berms

Berms are elevated masses of a mold of diverse shapes or an elevated barrier created with tightly packed soil. It is very useful in vertically disuniting pathways, forming road paths, and creating a fortification line in the army. It forms a good barrier for navigation, a good drainage system, and other beneficial purposes. It is also useful in temporarily holding water from an overflow, allowing stormwater to penetrate the soil, and providing an area to site plants for good ground cover.

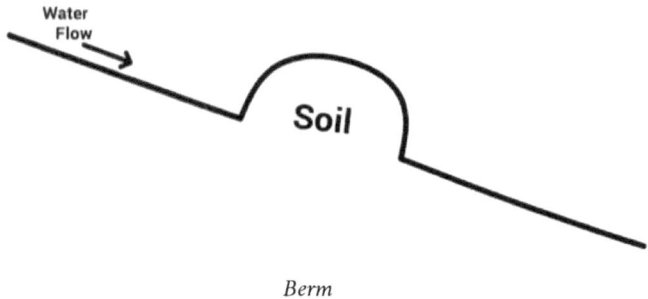

Berm

BASINS AND SWALES

A basin or swale is a shallow area of land that has been one of the oldest methods of managing stormwater in urban areas. You can create basins or swales to do the following;

I. Combat the problem of erosion that comes as a result of stormwater.

II. Temporarily receive harvested rainwater to recharge an aquifer after successful infiltration.

III. Direct rainwater your garden beds or plants to keep them hydrated.

III. Increase the fertility and quality of your soil texture.

Basins and swales are one of the easiest and quickest ways to make good use of rainwater. You don't want rainwater to pool in your garden beds, so it is best to build a swale either uphill or downhill of where you are growing your crops. If you are in a position where you can choose between the two, uphill is preferable. This way, rather than using a pump to move the water up to your garden, you can irrigate simply using the power of gravity, which is easier and cheaper.

Basins are shaped most times to resemble a bowl, while swales are constructed to be shaped in diverse crescent lines. The purpose of a basin is to receive water that was diverted away from another structure, such as a house or large building. Swales not only receive water that has been diverted, but they also function to move water to a different location.

I. Grass Swale

Grass Swale

This type of swale can be described as a channel constructed with soil and lined with grasses. This unique design guides and filters stormwater runoff from a collection of small drainages. They can be sited on roads, highways, and in residential areas. Grass swales have distinct features, which include free and stiff grass blades, thick coverage, and are hydrophilic to standing water. Grass swales eliminate pollutants mainly by filtration and sedimentation. They also remove inorganic and organic pollutants by accumulating and absorbing nutrients.

II. Wet Swale

Wet Swale

Wet swales look like grass swales, except they are constantly filled with water. Wet swales have attributes and functions similar to wetlands, constructed to thrive in linear environments. Grass swales contain elements such as dense vegetation, compact soil, and heavy hydration. They encourage filtration of stormwater runoff and take up a higher amount of nutrients than other types of swales due to the large plant population. Another amazing function of the wet swale is that they create conditions that favor anaerobic processes, encouraging nitrification and denitrification, thereby regulating the amount of nitrogen in the soil.

III. Infiltration Basins

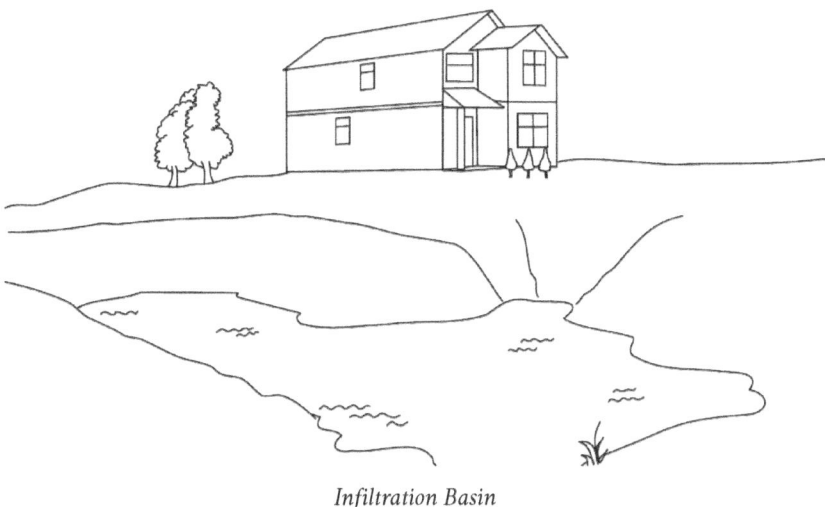

Infiltration Basin

These are excavated from a soil surface to form a basin-like structure. They are situated close to roads or buildings to receive stormwater. This is very helpful to keep roads from flooding and making driving hazardous or pooling water damaging the foundation of buildings. They also act to combat erosion by keeping water close to where it falls.

FRENCH DRAINS

A heavy storm or rainfall usually leads to the formation of stormwater which can accumulate at various points to form an unpleasant area of stagnant water. This can result in flooding or massive breeding of mosquitoes. This stagnant water also poses dire risks to your home's foundation. A french drain can be constructed and sited to guide the flow of stormwater runoff away from your house or land area.

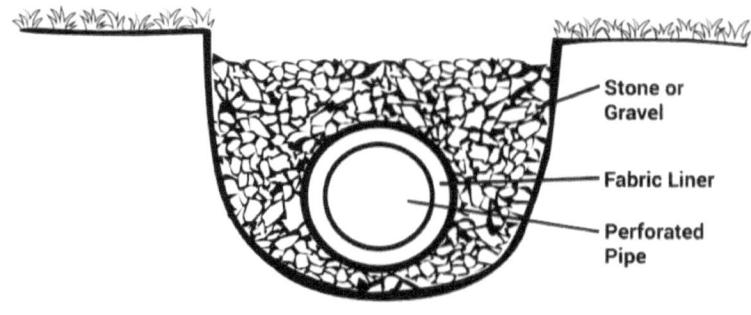

French Drain

A french drain can be described as a trench excavated from the ground in areas prone to floods due to severe stormwater runoff. A perforated pipe is lined with a fabric that can absorb water. This pipe is placed in the hole and the hole is then filled with several layers of gravel or stone. French drains function with the help of gravity that encourages water to flow downhill. The stormwater flows without hindrance into a strategically placed drain or other water drainages.

You might wonder why a perforated pipe is incorporated into the french drain and why a water-permeable fabric is usually wrapped around it. This is because the perforations on the pipe effectively collect and direct stormwater runoff from a flooded area to a drainage point. The pipe should be wrapped to discourage weeds, debris, and the like from blocking the perforations in the pipe.

TERRACES

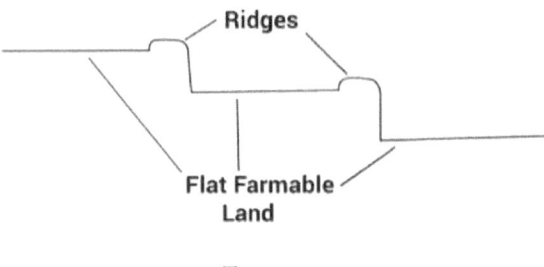

Terrace

A terrace turns a difficult to cultivate slope into flat farmable land with ridges. These areas resemble steps or a staircase. They reduce erosion from stormwater runoff and preserve moisture and nutrients for the production of crops. Terraces function to conserve both soil and water. They also make it possible for people in mountainous areas to productively farm land that would otherwise be unusable for farming. The ridges slow the flow of water down hill so it can infiltrate the ground. If you live in a dry region or area prone to dry spells, a terrace can increase the water available to your plants.

The process of rainwater harvesting is not limited to a single method. The foundation of each method starts with the eight principles of rainwater harvesting. But as far as how to specifically implement the process on your property, there are many diverse, fun, and creative ways you can catch rainwater.

4

END GOAL AND FEASIBILITY

T he beautiful and inspiring story of how three game changers turned a garbage yard into a world-class park is worth telling. This is the story of Mahim Nature Park, in Mumbai. This landscape, one of the most beautiful green areas, was once a wasteland and a dumping ground for over a hundred metric tons of garbage across Mumbai. Unfortunately, due to the rising pollution, the park was completely shut down in 1977.

A few years later, three individuals who resided in Mumbai and worked under the world wildlife fund decided to turn this wasteland into a beautiful Greenland. These three individuals are Salim Ali, a naturalist and ornithologist; Shanta Chatterji, the chairman of WWF and a corporate lawyer; and Himanshu Joshi, an educational officer. These three individuals intelligently actualized Greenland's vision for recreational and educational purposes.

The most interesting fact about the Mahim Nature Park is that since its inception, the park has completely depended on its own source of water supply and not on the general civic water supply. This was achieved by using the 15,070 square feet (1,400 square meters) roof of the main office building and the 2,150 square feet (200 square meters) courtyard as a catchment area for rainwater. This harvested rainwater is then directed to a large pond, where it is stored and distributed around the park throughout the year.

Though converting this wasteland into a park wasn't pleasant, the team was able to turn garbage into natural fertilizer for the vegetation. Due to their impressive work, the Mahim Nature Park is home to beautiful trees, an extensive population of butterflies, amphitheaters, libraries, research institutes, and a thriving tourist attraction site.

HOW MUCH WATER DO YOU NEED?

To determine the quantity of water you need in a day, it is important to identify and assess how you will use your daily water supply. We use water daily for bathing, doing the dishes, doing the laundry, gardening, cooking, for pets, flushing, and so much more.

You can use online water use calculators to effectively determine the amount you need to manage your rainwater harvesting project. I like the online water calculator on Southwest Florida's Water Management District's website:

https://www.swfwmd.state.fl.us/conservation/water-use-calculator

Here you estimate the number of times your family uses water for different purposes per day. You can also assess your household water use by looking at your water bill. Keep in mind that most people see fluctuations in their water use throughout the year. Of course, year-round, you're going to bathe, so that usage should stay about the same. But the amount of water you use to water your garden, wash your car, or let the kids run through the sprinklers will rise in the warm weather and lower when it's cold. So, it's best to look at your water usage over the course of a year rather than just the most recent month.

IS IT LEGAL?

The application of rainwater harvesting in Caribbean countries has helped provide a steady water supply even after being plagued by terrible hurricanes like Maria and Irma. Hurricanes Maria and Irma not only claimed people's homes, food, and lives, but there was also a severe lack of water supply for several months.

It will interest you to know that even before some Caribbean islands faced life-threatening hurricanes, there was a lack of a steady supply of clean potable water suitable for domestic uses. This lack was mainly due to the inability of the general utility water system to reach rural areas, or the water was too expensive for low-income families. Instead, these areas relied on streams, wells, and springs. The major downside to these water sources is the presence of contaminants or pollutants generated from domestic wastes or sewage.

To solve this pollution problem, rainwater harvesting system principles were adopted. Dominica can receive an average of fifteen inches of rainfall every month, which is quite a lot. Residents turned their roofs and sidewalks into catchment areas. They channeled this water to a storage tank or container with filters and water purifiers for domestic and commercial purposes like cooking, bathing, laundry, farming, and manufacturing.

I believe the idea of conceptualizing the process of installing a rainwater harvesting system must be exciting to you because of the numerous benefits attached to this process. It will help if you check out the laws that are considered binding in the environment where you live. Some countries encourage or even require rainwater harvesting because it provides people, especially in drought-prone areas, with a supply of water even when a municipality's supply may run low and threaten the ability of all to have clean water. On the other hand, some places prohibit harvesting rainwater due to the belief that water runoffs meant for lowlands would be hijacked by those living on the highlands, thereby causing severe water lack in the lowlands during drought.

The regulation on harvesting rainwater began way back in the gold rush era when miners went across the country in search of Californian streams suitable for them to dredge gold, which is the process of separating gold from gravel. To speed up the process, miners began to use a method called hydraulic mining, which started to pose serious negative effects on regions that barely got enough rainfall annually. To further increase their drive for mining gold, miners started digging channels that would divert water from faraway sources to their land area. This method brought about the principle or concept of prior appropriation, which signifies that the first person to create a channel or canal was entitled to the water that was successfully diverted: in layman's terms, "first come, first served."

This concept changed people's ideology about water, making water to be recognized as a unique property. Your ownership of a particular land area does not mean that you own the water. This rule has survived until this very moment in certain countries.

Benefits of Rainwater Harvesting Being Legal

Places that encourage harvesting rainwater have recorded immense benefits to their economy and the general status of their environment. These states have recorded increased civil water supply, energy conservation, and greater returns on rainwater harvesting systems. Houses have depended less on the main water supply, helping them save costs and relieve the stress of settling heavy water bills. Harvesting rainwater will also favor families when there is a clampdown on water use during drought.

Harvested rainwater is a useful backup for areas that lack a constant water supply. Also, having a functional rainwater harvesting system ensures you have enough water to combat fire outbreaks without waiting for water supply from fire hydrants.

Imprisoned for Harvesting a Little Water?

I have to tell you the unimaginable story of 64-year-old Gary Harrington, who was sentenced to thirty days imprisonment in 2016 for the illegal siphoning of rainwater on his large property in Oregon. This story made for effective clickbait for websites wanting to shock people with the absurd notion that someone minding his own business on his own land could be imprisoned for something so small. Well, that's not quite what actually happened. His imprisonment was largely based on the massive volume of water he collected. He harvested nearly 13 million gallons of water. That's enough to fill about twenty Olympic-size pools. He used that water to make large reservoirs where he built multiple docks and went out on his boats to recreationally fish the trout and bluegill he introduced into the reservoirs. Therefore the major reason for his arrest was for his diverting water that was meant to protect the environment, especially during drought.

I tell you this story not because I love when the government regulates what you can do on your own property, because I don't. I tell you this story because I want to give you a fair explanation of why rainwater harvesting is or is not legal and let you make your own decision if you think it's right or wrong. Many sources only tell you one side of the story. They only tell you the side that makes you furious with government fat-cats who act like they own the water that lands on your property. To give you a fair explanation of the topic, I have to show you the merits of both sides. Should people have the right to use rainwater that falls on their own property for the betterment of their and their family's lives? On the other hand, are there certain situations where the government should intervene when people take this to excess and bring harm to others downstream? With a level head and facts that accurately represent both sides, you are capable of making your own decision.

Legality Around the World

Australia

In Australia, the government has implemented some rules and incentives in some parts of the country to encourage rainwater harvesting. Installation of rainwater tanks in the new constructions of homes and business is now mandatory in many states. The government adopted this development to eliminate the disastrous effects of drought in the country.

England

Harvesting rainwater in England is encouraged, but you might need a license to combine harvested rainwater alongside any watercourse, gravity intake, land drainages, or underground strata. You are also not permitted to harvest so much water that it might diminish the amount of groundwater.

Canada

Canadians are free to harvest rainwater, but there are regulations around the practice. Generally, it is limited to non-potable use, such as fire prevention and flushing toilets. Also, if the system is not built up to code, the homeowner could be ticketed. Each province has slightly different regulations, but they are not well defined, and they leave a blurry line between who does and does not own the water.

Brazil

Brazil came up with a stunning project in 2003 to mitigate the prevalence of irregular rainfall. This project was called "Programa Um Milhão de Cisternas" ("One Million Cisterns"). The outstanding objective of this project was to provide approximately one million homes with a rooftop rainwater collection system to maximize the advantages of having an alternative source of water supply and cope well during periods of drought.

Singapore

Another country that has taken the lead in spearheading rainwater harvesting is Singapore. Despite its abundance of water, the country still struggled to meet its population's clean water demand. Even though Singapore receives a sufficient amount of rainfall annually, much of it was lost due to the country's restricted land area, which limited the amount of rainwater that could be collected. This was so much of a struggle that the country had to rely on the water supply from Malaysia to augment its own needs.

So, to curb the growing water stability concern, Singapore has focused its attention on water optimization through rainwater and flood control. The project involved the creation of an extensive network of canals and drains with a span of almost 5,000 miles (8000 km). Not only has this reduced the amount of flood-prone areas by almost 98% in 4 decades, but it redirects water that previously harmed its citizens to now be beneficially used for household purposes and drinking.

USA

There is a lot of conflicting information out there about if rainwater harvesting is legal or not across the US. The reason for this is that not too long ago, it was illegal in some states, such as Colorado and Utah. In Utah, it was actually considered theft from the state to harvest rainwater on your property until 2010. Such laws have since been updated, and it is now legal in all states to harvest rainwater. Some states, such as Ohio, Illinois, and Georgia, allow it but have placed restrictions on the practice. This is due to either concern water will be taken away from those downstream or fear citizens will not properly clean and tend to their systems, which will result in disease. Other states, such as Florida, Rhode Island, and Virginia, encourage it with various tax incentives because they view it as beneficial for conservation and reducing demand on the state's water supply.

Figuring out your water needs and the regulations or possible tax incentives attached to a rainwater harvesting system in the area you live is the first thing to consider before starting the exciting journey of harvesting rainwater. The next thing to consider is what components will be necessary for your system.

5

DEBRIS REMOVAL DEVICES

K enya, an African country that experienced drought in recent years, stood the test of time and improved its food production this past few years by taking advantage of the rain harvesting system. Farmers in Kenya who made use of the rain harvesting system have experienced a substantial increase in their food production.

Food crops grown only in the rainy season are now being produced in the dry season by water that is stored and covered in mulches that absorb this water supply to prevent it from being dried off. The water supply is redirected from the road, filling the ponds or drums kept in different locations underground. The rain harvesting system in Kenya provides an excellent solution for farmers in arid or semi-arid regions, such as Makueni. Funds are also provided for farmers by some operations such as the Alliance For a Green

Revolution in Africa, and the Drylands Development Program.

REMOVING DEBRIS

Why use debris removal devices?

Debris removal devices vary in size. Some function to keep large items out of your main storage tank, such as leaves and sticks, while others include filters with tiny holes as small as 280-440 microns. This means that only tiny grain of sand size particles can pass through. One reason you should install a debris removal device is to filter off biological debris that provides food and nutrients for existing bacteria in the water storage tank. This biological debris promotes harmful bacteria growth and thereby contaminates the water. Debris that is not well filtered goes on to settle at the bottom of your water storage tank.

Debris that is large enough can block the pipes in the conveyance systems and creates extra work or expenses to unclog or clear the pathway. They also substantially increase the cost of filtering and purifying the rainwater supply. Sometimes it can also render the whole amount of water stored useless. When the water is overly concentrated with debris, organic matter, algae, and other harmful bacteria, it will have an awful smell, and it won't be useful for personal use anymore. Having this problem and the increased work it causes can quickly erode your enthusiasm for creating your own water supply. Don't let that happen to you!

Ways To Remove Debris From Harvested Water

Harvesting clean rainwater is the end goal of a rain harvester. Clean rainwater can be used for numerous purposes like cooking, drinking, and sanitary needs; the list is endless. But this rainwater that is being harvested isn't always clean. Rainwater at the beginning of a rain event is mixed up with different substances from the air, such as dust or smoke particles that bind to the rainwater. It falls on your rooftop and still meets other particles and pathogens that add to it. People use various ways to remove debris from harvested water, but I will be talking about just a few of the most important ways I find to be most effective.

Gutter Mesh

This is a mesh placed over your gutter that prevents unwanted elements from entering your water supply. This step is very effective. The type of gutter screen I recommend is between the seamless aluminum gutter or a gutter with a drop-in-lasting mesh built to meet the requirements of the ANSI/NSF standard 14/61.

Unwanted elements that fall into your gutters, such as leaves, feces, and carcasses, can prevent the passage of rainwater into your down sprout, automatically causing a reduction in the amount of water that flows into your water storage tanks. These undesirables also provide favorable conditions for other bacteria in the water storage tank, promoting algae growth. Leaves and other solid materials can also clog your pipes; thereby causing an increase in expenses and labor.

Feces of animals can also get washed into your storage tank if a gutter mesh isn't installed in your rain harvesting system. This affects your home as the stored water would later emit bad odors and be an ideal breeding ground for those annoying and sometimes deadly insects: mosquitoes.

Cleaning out your gutters should become part of your routine. They should be cleaned at the beginning of the rainy season to remove all unwanted elements that might have clogged them to ensure free passage of the rainwater. If you don't clean your gutters before the rain, you will likely get less rainwater into your storage tank because debris and other sediments will absorb or block the water. If not removed quickly enough, all the leftover filtered debris serves as breeding grounds for mosquitoes and cooties.

Rain Screens

Getting a rain screen is a great addition to your rainwater harvesting system. Rain screens are not located on the rooftop was with gutter screens. Rather, rain screens are located a few inches below the downspout. They can be made from any metal, depending on your preferences.

The best rain screens are built in a 45-degree position, which allows for easy sliding off of debris. The edges of rain screens are slightly raised to prevent water from overpouring, and the mesh covering is tiny enough to keep out debris and insects.

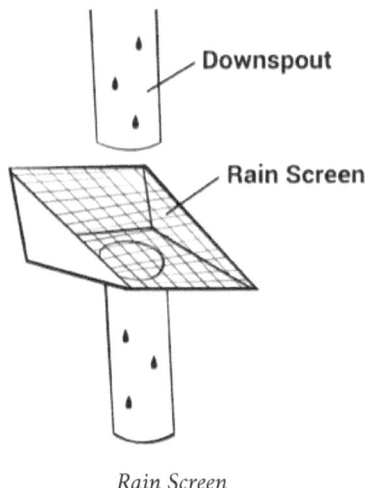

Rain Screen

Since they aren't built on the rooftop, it's easier to maintain. A good amount of the debris will slide off on its own, and any materials that remain can easily be seen. Gutter mesh debris can become an "out of sight, out of mind" problem, but with rain screens, you're more likely to see it and thus more likely to quickly fix the issue. Another benefit is they do not promote water puddles, and thus mosquitoes.

FIRST FLUSH DIVERTER

The Diverter (FFD) is a device that is used to divert the first and dirtiest polluted rainwater collected from rooftops. One of the amazing things about rainfall is that it purifies the air.

This is an extremely valuable function of rain, but keep in mind that those pollutants don't just disappear. You'll find them in the first 0.02 to 0.03 inch (0.5 to 0.75 mm) of a rain event.

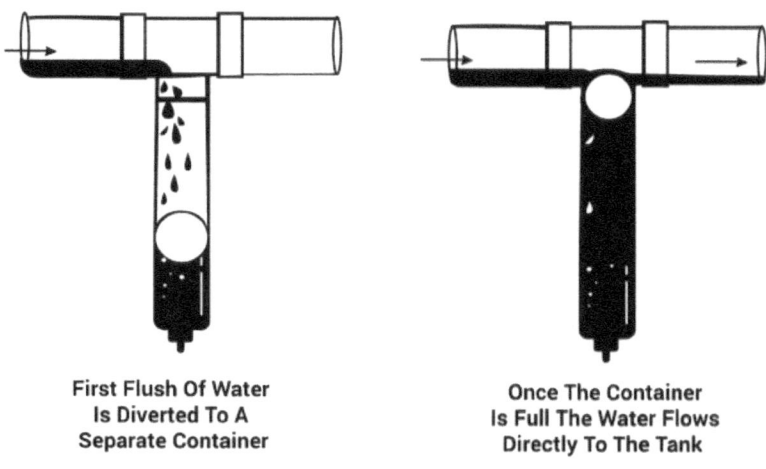

First Flush Of Water
Is Diverted To A
Separate Container

Once The Container
Is Full The Water Flows
Directly To The Tank

First Flush Diverter

The first flush diverter also collects the debris that has gathered on the rooftop between rainfalls. Harmful materials can be picked up from a roof, or any other catchment that is used, such as toxins, pathogens, bacteria, and other unwanted substances. They are primarily used to prevent soluble pollutants or fine suspended solids like pollen or crickets from entering the water storage tank.

The amount of water that should be diverted into the first flush diverter depends on the following factors:

- Amount and size of debris on the rooftop:
- Fecal matter or heavy waste like dead animals are harder to be flushed than dust or light debris. Note that the amount of debris increases as the time between rainfall increases.
- Intensity of the rainfall:
- If the rainfall intensity is low, debris is slow to be washed off the rooftop.
- Rooftop materials:
- Metal-like materials will clean faster than non-metals or porous materials.

How A First Flush Diverter Works

As rain falls, wetting your roof space, the particles on the roof, such as leaves, microorganisms, insects, dust, and other small particles, get washed down with the rain. When rain falls, and the first batch of rain supply goes down the pipe, the diverter gets filled first then the cleaner rain supply goes into the main storage.

Once the diverter is full, it closes up by a ball at the bottom of the diverter floating towards the surface to block the entrance. The first flush diverter function is to prevent the entry of these particles into the main water supply and prevent the blockage of pipes by large size debris. After the rain storm is over, you can open the bottom of the first flush diverter to empty the contents, and it will be ready for the next rain.

The amount of water that should be diverted can vary depending on the factors we just discussed, but as a general guideline, studies show that at least 10 gallons (38 liters) of water per 1000 square feet (93 square meters) of catchment area should go into the first flush diverter. However, if your roof is particularly dirty due to the material of your roof, the length of time between rains, or if you live in an area with a lot of pollution, it would be a good idea to add a couple of gallons to that number.

Advantages Of A First Flush Diverter

1. Debris and other large particles that don't get removed from the water and go to the water storage tank have a probability of blocking the pipes and spouts.

2. Water gathered from the beginning of a rainfall event is filled with bugs and other sediments from the roof. If not removed, the big particles can accumulate into algae and make your stored water dirty.

3. Making use of the first flush diverter also increases the life span of your pumps and other appliances in your rainwater harvesting system.

4. They help to reduce time spent on tank maintenance.

5. First flush diverters decrease the cost of filtering the rainwater supply.

6. As rainwater purifies the air at the beginning of a rainfall, particles that are not good for our health can mix with water droplets in the air and as a result pose a threat to humans. First rain may simply contain dust and pollen, but in areas with heavier pollution, you may find toxic heavy metals in the rainwater. How much or how little pollutants are in the first rain depends on the air quality in your area. I recommend testing your water, especially if you plan to use it as your drinking water source.

When Not To Use A First Flush Diverter

- When you cannot size them correctly

Getting the first flush diverter sized correctly can be difficult. It depends on factors such as the amount of rain, the difference in time between rainfall, wind intensity, wind direction, and rooftop area. The first flush size, if too big, leads to wastage of the rainwater, and too little still makes the pathogens and particles that were meant to be diverted away enter your main storage supply.

Another difficulty with this is that other factors interfere with predicting the amount of water that needs to be diverted. For example, if the last rainfall was two days ago and another rain is falling today, the water that needs to be diverted using the first flush diverter should be less than if the difference between the last rainfall was days, weeks, or even months! If you follow the above example and divert a small amount of water because the time between rains is short, what if there was high wind speed in an area with excess dry leaves? The amount of dirt on your roof will increase substantially more than someone not living in a windy area and surrounded by leaves, even though the length of time between the last rain and the present was small.

- If you do not have time for the maintenance

The first flush diverter needs the right maintenance to effectively prevent damaging your system. The first flush diverter should be assessed for leaks and damages before and after rainfall. The previous rain's first flush should be drained after every rain, and the dirt trapped in the filter should also be removed and thrown away.

- Create a weak point in the conveyance system

First flush diverters are made out of plastic and are exposed to harsh conditions. A heavy storm or freezing temperature can cause leaks or burst pipes, leading to increased wastage of water that was meant to be stored. Damage to the first flush diverter prevents the rainwater from entering your storage tank.

- Presence of organic matter in the rain supply

Research has shown that the first flush in areas with few pollutants in the air is a low-grade fertilizer that's good for your plants or flowers. If you intend to use the water collected for farming purposes, should this low-grade fertilizer be disposed of or used? Most people who use their stored water don't see the need for a first flush diverter because they claim it is useful. This can be a crossroads if you intend to use your stored water for personal and gardening purposes. I would advise running your first flush into a barrel or any other water storage equipment which you can have access to when you wish to use this low-grade fertilizer for your flowers or crops. The microbes and other organic materials gathered on the roof are beneficial for the crops. If your main purpose is storing water is for irrigation, why should these useful organic materials be thrown away?

- Small volume of rainfall

Many farmers or people who desperately need the rain harvesting system do not have the luxury of disposing of the first flush. People living in dry regions that experience very little rainfall do not have the luxury of diverting any of this away. They would mostly filter it manually or by sieving.

- When you still need to screen the water

Most, if not all, people screen their water supply before use. Some people would say that if this will later remove the debris and particles that are unfit for water storage, why bother diverting the first flush?

At the end of the day, what really matters is that you use the rainwater harvesting system that works best for you and your needs. There's no point in doing all the work to research, buy parts, and install a system if you're not going to be happy with it and won't use it. If the first flush diverter makes sense for your situation, use it. If any of the above reasons apply to you and it would not be beneficial for you, don't use it. That's the beauty of having your own system. You get to do it your way.

6

LET'S GET DOWN TO BUSINESS

Ayyappa Masagi, a native of a small village in Northern Karnataka, India, is widely recognized as a water warrior, a water magician, and a water Gandi. He earned these titles by applying water conservation principles to solving India's problem of water scarcity. Growing up, Ayyappa Masagi would daily walk miles to get water for his family. This fueled his passion for water conservation. He worked to gain applicable knowledge about agriculture and water supply with the help of his parents and thorough research. After graduating, he began his journey as a mechanical engineer for twenty-three years, after which he quit his job and established a foundation known as the Water Literacy Foundation to help India solve its problem of water scarcity.

Ayyappa Masagi was famous for his ability to save the fortunes of thousands of people by convincing them to harvest and conserve rainwater. He started this water conservation journey by purchasing a six-acre land in a small Gadag village located in a dry region with low rainfall. He then planted cash crops like coffee and rubber to prove that it was possible to grow any crop in any location as long as there was a steady source of water supply. For about two years, he recorded huge success, but unfortunately, he lost all his crops due to severe drought in the following year. This spurred mockery from people around him, but he was not fazed and kept up his determination to find a lasting solution. He converted his farm into his research center and studied the rainfall pattern. After proper research, he created a rainwater harvesting system that is pit based and made of gravel, boulders, sand, and mud. With this system of rainwater harvesting in place, he was able to recharge aquifers and solve problems arising from water scarcity.

Interestingly, people who mocked him and accused him of wasting precious time began to hold both him and his project in high esteem. They started learning from him and adopting the process of rainwater harvesting in their homes. Ayyappa Masagi knew that he was on to something when he started this process and because he didn't give up when it got hard, he ended up making a meaningful and lasting difference.

The process of harvesting rainwater is both exciting and satisfying. In this very informative chapter, I will get the ball rolling by teaching you how you can capture the delicate raindrops from the sky above your roof and channel the precious gift of nature to your preferred storage system so you can maximize its full benefits! I can assure you that after applying the principles and procedures explained in this chapter, your garden will stay green and fresh all year round.

I'm going to go over a few different kinds of rainwater harvesting systems, varying from simple to quite complex. Read through these to get a better understanding of what you can do with your system, but choose which to install on your site based on what will be best for you. We all have different water needs and rainwater harvesting goals. If right now you are only looking to water a small backyard garden with your system or if the complexities of the more intricate systems are overwhelming, start off with rain barrels. You can always upgrade later. However, if you are that all-or-nothing type of person who is determined to dive 100% all in, go for it! Do your research, and then get that rainwater harvesting system you've been dreaming of!

RAIN BARRELS

Collecting into a rain barrel is great for beginners or for those who only want to collect a small amount for watering a small garden or lawn. You can buy rain barrels from many hardware stores. One of the really nice things about these is that they usually come with all of the pieces you need, and components, like a spigot or overflow spout, are already included.

Step 1: Pick the most favorable spot to site your rain barrel.

The best place to fix your rain barrel is below your gutter downspout, which carries stormwater from your property to a more suitable place. Also, be sure to fix your rain barrel on flat ground that is even on all sides to prevent the barrel from spilling its contents. In cases where you wish to irrigate your garden or lawn with the harvested water in your rain barrel, choose a gutter downspout closest to the garden or area of land lacking in water supply. If the water doesn't have to travel as far, this will make it easier to get the water where you want it to be.

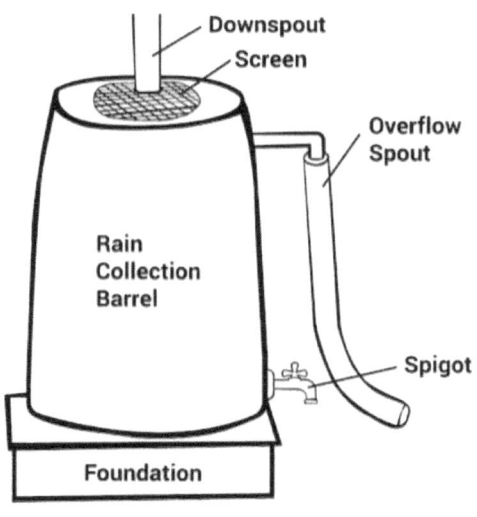

Rain Barrel

Step 2: Start your foundation.

After figuring out the best spot to site your rain barrel, you can prepare your foundation sites in two ways:

1. Elevation Platform: To increase water pressure and flow rate from your rain barrel, you can place it on an elevated platform which should be strong enough to bear the weight of three hundred pounds of water-filled rain barrels. Two of the easiest materials to make these foundations out of are wood pallets or cinder blocks.

2. Gravel or sand pit: In place of a platform, you can dig a pit two to three inches deep, then fill it with sand or gravel and smooth the top to bring out a flat ground on which to sit the rain barrel. Installing your rainwater on a platform is best if you wish to use it along with a drip irrigation system.

Step 3: Install a screen.

Rain barrels come with a hole in the top to allow for the venting of air as water fills up or flows out of the container. Depending on the design of the barrel, it may be the same hole where water enters from the downspout or these could be two separate holes. If you leave a vent hole open, all kinds of things could get it, such as leaves, bugs, and small animals. Curious children could also throw random objects into the barrel just to see what happens. (All the parents and grand-parents of young children know what I'm talking about.) That is why it is a good idea to secure a screen over that opening.

Step 4: Cut the downspout and place the barrel.

Place your rain barrel next to your downspout so that you can see at what length you will need to cut the downspout. Mark where your cut should be, then use a hacksaw to do the job. After that is done, you can move your rain barrel directly under the downspout. If you see that the length of the downspout is not exactly where you want it, now is the time to make adjustments. Once your barrels start collecting rain, they will become very heavy, and adjustments will be more difficult to make.

Step 5: Direct the spigot and overflow valve away from your house.

After fixing your rain barrel on the foundation you have created, ensure you direct the overflow valve and the spigot away from your house to have convenient access to a steady water supply and to allow the overflow valve to transport water that is not needed away from your house's foundation.

Step 6: Use the water.

To direct your harvested rainwater to where it needs to go, fix a hose or pipe to the spigot attached to your rain barrel and direct the flow to your garden for watering. Another option is to bring your watering can directly to your rain barrel and fill it with water from the spigot.

IBC TOTES

IBCs, also known as intermediate bulk containers, are mostly used commercially for storing harmful chemicals or industrial liquids. You can also use them to store huge quantities of rainwater. These tanks are portable with various designs to choose from and cost-effective due to their durability. These will usually hold up well against the elements for over 10 years.

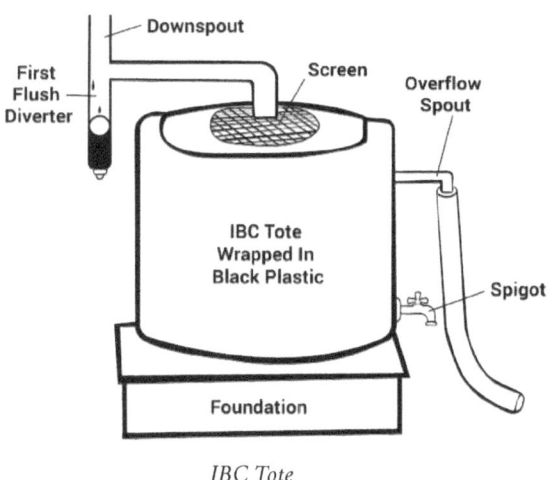

IBC Tote

Step 1: Block the light.

After purchasing your intermediate bulk containers, you should first wrap them completely in thick black plastic or polyethylene to prevent light from entering the containers, thereby discouraging the formation of unpleasant algae.

Step 2: Make a foundation.

Much of this installation process is similar to rain barrels. Next, you will need to choose a proper location and make a foundation under your downspout. This can be done in either method option for rain barrels, but it will need to be bigger since IBC totes are much larger than the rain barrels that are generally on sale at hardware stores.

Step 3: Install a screen.

IBC totes will come with a hole on top that is usually covered with a screw-on cap. You will take the cap off and install a screen in its place. This will serve as both a vent and an area where water will flow in from your downspout.

Step 4: Install pre-storage filters.

You will need to cut your downspout to the appropriate length, and if you have chosen to use a first flush diverter or rain screen, this is a good time to install them. Both can be purchased from many hardware stores or online. If you want mesh installed on your gutters, you can do that prior to starting the IBC tote installation process. Keep in mind that installing gutter mesh is going to take some time, especially if your house is more than one story. So, plan for installing gutter mesh and your IBC tote to take a good amount of the day or make it into a two-day process.

Step 5: Direct the overflow.

When placing the IBC tote on the foundation, be sure to direct the spigot and overflow spout away from your house's foundation.

Step 6: Use the water.

You can still fill up a watering can or connect a hose to the spigot to move the water when you want to use it. But if you are harvesting this much water, you may need it to reach farther away from your system, so you'll need more water pressure. If that is the case, a water pump will be a great addition to your rainwater harvesting system. Many hardware stores sell solar-powered water pumps. You may also be interested in checking out products made by companies specializing in rainwater harvesting. These companies will probably be harder to find locally, but you can go online and search for rainwater harvesting supply companies.

UNDERGROUND CISTERNS

Cisterns are one of the larger water storage tank options and can be placed above or underground. Due to their large size, many homeowners prefer to have them buried underground to save space and avoid the eyesore. Another great benefit of keeping your water source underground is that your cistern will be insulated from the cold and, therefore, usable even in freezing temperatures. These can be made with various materials, including concrete, steel, fiberglass, or polyethylene. I'll focus in-depth on how to choose the right material for your cistern in the next chapter. If you want a high-capacity rainwater harvesting system that can provide water for both your outdoor needs and in-home needs, including drinking water, this is for you.

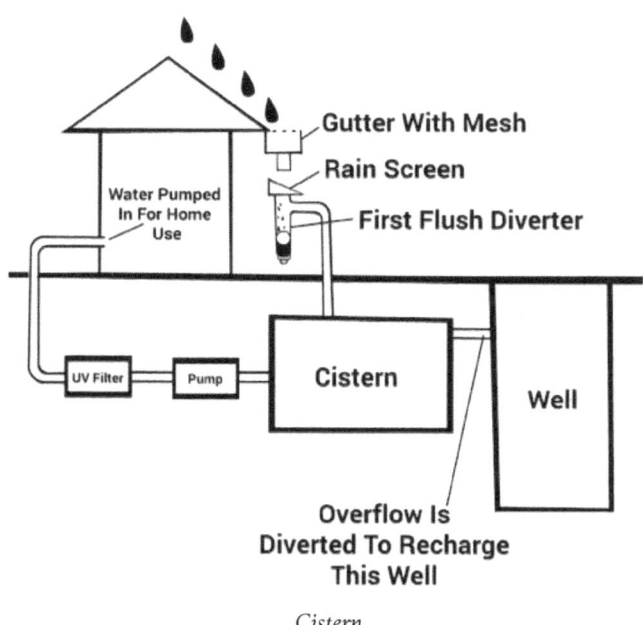

Cistern

Before I get into the steps for installing an underground cistern, I have to say this one is quite an undertaking. You can do it yourself, but you will need heavy equipment and technical expertise. I take a lot of pride and satisfaction in doing things myself and do most things with my own two hands. This is one thing, though, that I recommend hiring a professional unless you have plumbing and heavy equipment experience.

Step 1: Excavate a place for the cistern.

You will need to dig a hole that is 2 feet (0.5 meter) longer, wider, and deeper than the size of the tank. These tanks come in different sizes, but any one you choose is going to be large enough that you'll want to use a backhoe to do the digging. Of course, you could dig this by hand, but...yikes. That's going to be a lot of digging.

Step 2: Fill the bottom and lower the tank.

Dump 5 inches (130 mm) of sand or gravel into the bottom of your hole and level it out. After that, your site is now prepared for the tank to be lowered into the hole. A crane will be necessary to handle the weight of moving a cistern.

Step 3: Install the water pump and filter.

Since you will need to move water against gravity, from underground to above, to be able to use your supply, you will need to install a pump. Also, since this water is going to be pumped into the house for potable use, it needs to be thoroughly filtered. Gutter mesh, rain screens, and first flush diverters all help to keep water clean, but if this water will be used for drinking, it will need an additional filter that is especially for making water drinkable. Common methods of making water clean enough to drink are chlorination, UV light, or ozonation. I'll go over each of those in more detail in the next chapter.

Step 4: Dig the waterline trench and connect to your home supply.

Dig far enough into the ground to be below your area's frost line. Once a trench has been dug between your water tank and home, you can lay pipes to connect the cistern to your home's water supply.

Step 5: Cover the tank.

Fill in the empty space on the sides of the tank with sand or gravel. The tank can then be covered with soil and planted with grass seed or whatever shallow root vegetation you would like to grow there. This is not a good place for anything that will develop large and deep roots because that could damage your cistern.

CONNECTING TWO OR MORE TANKS

You can decide to increase your rainwater harvesting storage capacity by maximizing the use of two or more tanks. The perfect way of utilizing these tanks effectively is to link the tanks together. There are two major ways of linking two or more tanks, either from the top or bottom.

Linking two or more tanks from the top ensures that each tank gets filled up with rainwater one at a time in a way that harvested rainwater flows from the overflow of the first tank into the top opening of the second tank. To ensure accurate connection, the principle of gravity must be maintained by making the overflow channel of the first tank a little bit higher than the inlet of the second tank. Also, ensure that the two tanks are of the same height and size. Linking two or more tanks from the bottom employs a method that makes all tanks in the rainwater harvesting system fill simultaneously and at the same level.

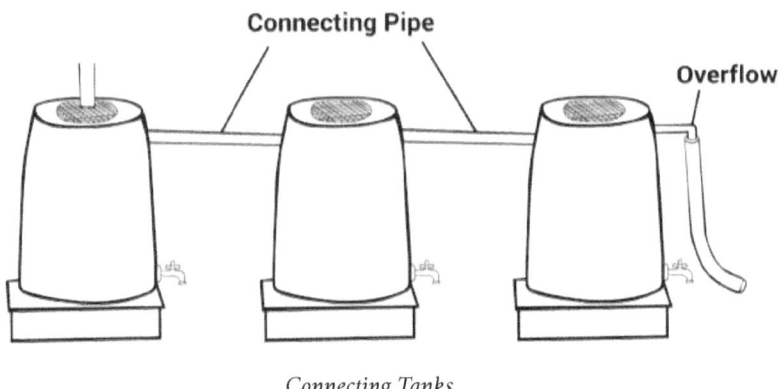

Connecting Tanks

You can use this technique to connect two cisterns, but it is more commonly used to connect smaller tanks such as IBC totes or rain barrels. I've seen a lot of people do this when they want to start rainwater harvesting with a small system, but after the first year, they really like their results and want to increase their storage capacity. Connecting an additional tank or multiple tanks is a great way to increase your storage without having to make major changes in your system.

Another great benefit of using multiple tanks is that the first tank acts as a settling tank.

After rain falls on your roof, goes through your pipes and filters, and lands in your storage tank, there will still be small particles of sediment, such as dirt and dust. The easiest way to separate that sediment from the rest of the water is to give it time to sit. The sediment is heavier than the rest of the water in the tank and will naturally sink to the bottom. When the water flows into the first tank, that is an opportunity for sediment that has been suspended in the water as it flowed through the conduits to fall to the bottom of the tank. Thus, most of the sediment will settle in the bottom of the first tank, leaving the next tank with cleaner water.

FOG CATCHMENT SYSTEM

What is a fog catchment system?

Fog catchment is the process of harvesting or capturing fog as an alternative water supply source in areas with high fog concentrations, such as mountainous and coastal regions. It employs harvesting systems designed in the form of a net fixed between two poles that spread out to capture wind that is carrying heavy fog. As the wind blows through the wire mesh, you will notice drops of fresh water forming and dripping into a collection container containing pipes transporting fresh water into a storage tank.

The fog collecting system is an unconventional practice, but it produces and fends for people living in high-drought areas like Chile and Peru. In Chile, there is a particular fog called Camanchacas, a thick fog that touches the ground. It is easily harvested by simple fog collecting tools.

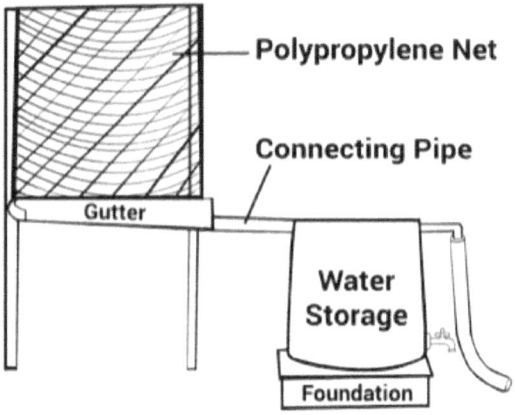

Fog Catchment

To "catch the fog," a mesh net made from nylon or polypropylene, rectangular and flat in shape, is spread out and tied to two supporting posts. This structure is placed perpendicular to the incoming fog; as the fog passes through, it captures tiny drops of water that coalesce and trickle down to the fog fence under the mesh net, which then flows to gutters or a tank. Sometimes government subsidies are used in getting the supplies for the fog collecting materials, and it's a community participation project.

+ Advantages of Fog Collecting Systems

- It is ecologically friendly, having no adverse effect on the ecosystem or environment.
- The expenses incurred to build and collect rain are very low.
- It is very easy to build.
- It requires no active energy to transport the water from the fog collecting site.
- There is little to no maintenance and expenses for repair to fog collectors.
- Reduces dependence on freshwater during low rainfall periods.

— Disadvantages of Fog Collecting Systems

- It can't yield large volumes of water supply.
- Locations where fog collection can take place are very limited.
- Setting up a fog collection system is not a one-person activity.
- Sometimes, though rare before the water trickles down to the settlement or town, it may sometimes be in an undrinkable state.

The fog harvesting method as an alternative to steady water supply during a drought has greatly benefited desert places like Chile. However, Chile does experience a season of favorable atmospheric conditions, which enhance the process of fog harvesting. Residents can take advantage of the fog-prone Andean slope to generate high water levels for domestic, industrial, agricultural and commercial purposes.

COLLECTING FROM SOLAR PANELS

On your journey to self-reliance, you may already have solar panels on your roof. If you have enough room, you may have even set aside a portion of land to fill with solar panels and make your own solar energy farm. In that case, I have good news. You can collect rainwater from solar panels too!

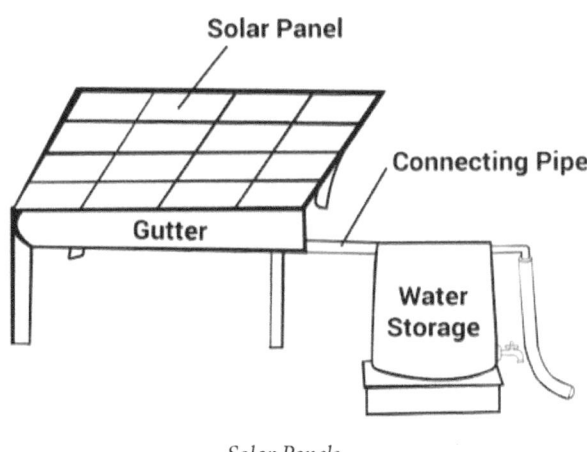

Solar Panels

Solar panels in a solar farm are a convenient catchment area because they are lower to the ground than a roof, and thus it's easier to attach rainwater harvesting system components. All you need to do is attach a gutter to the bottom of the solar panel that leads to a rainwater collection barrel. The downside of solar panels is that studies have shown the presence of lead and cadmium concentrations in the harvested water. So, it is advisable to use water harvested from solar panels for non-potable uses.

HOW TO DIY ON A TIGHT BUDGET

Suppose you find yourself in a situation whereby your budget does not seem to fit into the right rainwater harvesting system. In that case, you can bury your worries by paying rapt attention to ways to create your rainwater harvesting system completely on a low budget.

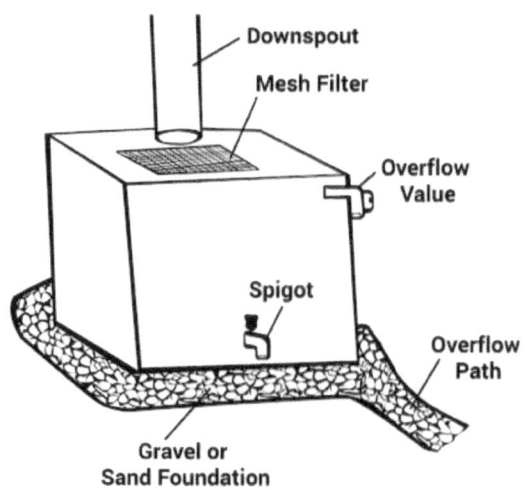

Rainwater Harvesting on a Budget

Step 1: Repurpose a storage container.

Get any storage container of your choice, depending on your budget, and clean this container thoroughly before use. Also, make sure the storage container does not permit light entry.

Step 2: Make a foundation.

Flatten the area next to your gutter downspout, and add a layer of gravel or sand to further assist the drainage system around your foundation and prevent water from pooling around your house.

Step 3: Add a spigot and overflow valve.

Create a hole a few inches from the bottom of your barrel and attach a spigot. Make a hole for an overflow valve pathway two inches below the top of the barrel. Position the overflow valve away from your house.

Step 4: Attach the downspout and mesh.

Cut a hole in the top of your container and cover it with mesh to keep out debris. Cut your downspout to the correct length and position your container on your foundation to collect the water from your downspout.

MANAGING FOR OVERFLOW

From time to time, you will receive more rainfall than what can fit in your collection container. This extra will flow out through your overflow spout, so it is wise to plan ahead for where you want this water to go. As we've talked about before, you do not want this water to go towards your house's foundation. If it's directed there and stays there for too long, it could damage the foundation, which is dangerous and costly to repair. However, there are other good places for this overflow to go. You can point it in the direction of a recharge structure to help refill an aquifer or you can take advantage of the extra water and make a rain garden.

Rain Garden

A rain garden is a fun way to take advantage of rainwater collection barrel overflow without feeling like the water that doesn't fit in your barrel is wasted. You can create a rain garden by digging out a small basin in the direction of your overflow. If your rain garden will be more than a few feet from your overflow valve, you can make sure this extra water flows to the correct area by attaching a conduit to the overflow valve that reaches all the way to your rain garden. To make it more visually appealing and avoid a tripping hazard, dig a trench between the barrel and rain garden to bury this pipe. Fill the low area with native plants that thrive in moisture-rich environments. Creating a rain garden serves two purposes. First, it is a way to increase the variety of plants you are able to cultivate on your land. Biodiversity is decreasing around the world, but this is a way you can combat that problem in your own backyard. Second, the plants in your rainwater garden act as a filter to clean the water, and the garden's basin shape slows the flow of water, which encourages it to infiltrate your soil rather than run off.

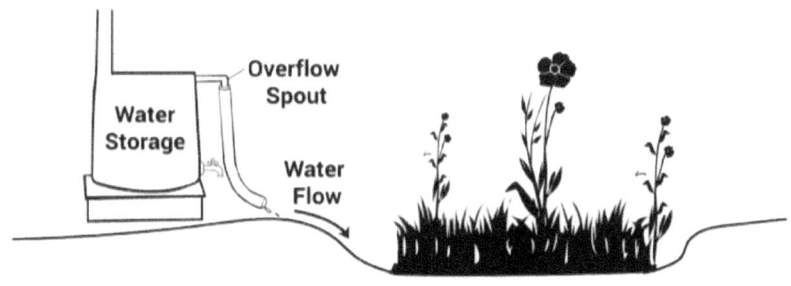

Rain Garden

There are many options to customize your rainwater harvesting system to make it exactly what you need. Which system makes the most sense for you and your water needs? You don't have to break the bank or empty your purse to install your rainwater harvesting system. You can build an effective system if you have saved $50 or $5,000.

7

RAINWATER STORAGE AND PURIFICATION

Necessity, they say, is the mother of invention, which has been proven by Mwema Maswili, a Kenyan farmer who, in 1998, engineered the invention of a runoff rainwater harvesting system. The incidence of low annual rainfall and poor soil fertility led him to create a roadside drain near a dust road with limited access. This rainwater harvesting system was later improved using contour strokes with technical application from peaceworkers in 2005; thereby solving the farming problems associated with drought and simultaneously increasing overall yield.

Now armed with the technology that comes with rainwater harvesting, many Kenyan farmers after experiencing years of drought, leading to food insecurity domestically, are now bouncing back with fruit orchards and bountiful harvests.

Just like Mwema Maswili, you can create your breakthrough rainwater conservation story.

STORAGE CONSIDERATIONS

Water storage tank materials

One of the good things about storing harvested rainwater is the availability of a wide range of storage tank options to suit your everyday household, industrial, and agricultural needs. As I would always say, the most important things to look out for when investing in storage tanks are size, quality, and durability.

Below I have outlined different materials from which storage tanks are made to help you in making your choice of what material will be best for you.

1. Steel

Corrosion is one major issue you will face with using steel water tanks because steel rusts and this metallic substance mixes with your water and gives it a metallic taste. To prevent this rust, they are coated with plastic on the inside to prevent corrosion. So, don't cross out getting a steel water tank from your list. They are among the oldest materials used to make tanks in the 70s and 80s, and they are what we often see in older buildings or sheds.

2. Fiberglass

Fiberglass is reinforced plastics with resin. Tanks made from fiberglass are relatively hard and highly resistant to damage. If you live in a very windy or high rainfall state or country, getting a tank made from fiberglass is one of the best choices you can make. They are anti-corrosive; they do not expand or react in extreme climate conditions, which makes them perfect for people living in countries with extreme climate conditions. Fiberglass tanks have a high lifespan of about 40 to 50 years which can make them both beneficial and limiting. Beneficial due to their high durability and limiting as a result of their being very hard to recycle.

Fiberglass is made from different chemical-inclined products, so this may not be a wise choice for you if you want to use the tank for potable water. Despite this, the good news is that it can be lined with a food-grade coating to prevent the chemical products from breaking away into the stored water.

Due to being a relatively light material, sunlight easily passes through it, promoting algae growth. Using it for an underground tank eradicates the light factor.

3. Polyethylene

Polyethylene is the most popular type of plastic. Tanks made from polyethylene are light and very easy to transport. If the mode of transportation is a huge factor for you when choosing materials for your water tanks, polyethylene-made tanks are the best. They can also add to the aesthetic feeling of your house because they come in different colors. If you are concerned about price, accessibility, corrosion, and damage, polyethylene ticks all these boxes.

You may think polyethylene is the best material to make your water tanks of, but it also has its disadvantages. They can be hard to recycle. They also promote algae growth because they are light, and sunlight can pass through them. They can get damaged easily, but they are also easy to repair. You can have your polyethylene water tank painted black to reduce or inhibit algae growth. Polyethylene water tanks can last for a minimum of 10 years.

4. Concrete

Concrete tanks can last up to 50 to 60 years. If you are interested in durability, concrete will provide that for you. Concrete-made tanks have a very high level of tolerance for harsh weather and fire. It can be weakened when exposed to these factors but not destroyed. They are easy to recycle and add to your property's aesthetic because you can make them in a color that matches or suits your surroundings.

If space is one of the factors you are concerned about in getting a water tank, concrete material used for water tanks provides a solution. Water tanks made of concrete can be placed above ground, but they are most commonly placed below ground, maybe under your driveway or backyard, thereby saving spacing. The can easily handle the weight of a lawnmower or cars. Keep in mind though, the heavy equipment used to install the concrete cistern may be too much for the concrete to bear. So, check with the manufacturer for your cistern's load bearing capacity before putting anything especially heavy on it.

Concrete tanks have some great benefits, but there are drawbacks too. Unfortunately, they are prone to creaks and leaks. So, though they will last a long time before breaking down enough to be unusable, it may not be long before it develops small leaks.

5. Stainless steel

Stainless steel material tanks are an option I highly recommend for personal use. It is so good it is used to store other resources apart from water. They are used in breweries, wine-making companies, rum, chocolates, and anything you can think of. Stainless steel is up to the task.

Stainless steel is made mainly out of chromium (a rare material) and less percentage of carbon and other alloy elements like nickel, manganese, and titanium, which amplify its corrosion resistance and durability. Many people highly prefer tanks made out of stainless steel. I can relate to why because of their numerous advantages and safe properties. They are very durable, resistant, and can last up to 50 years because of their alloy elements. Their inner layer is coated with chromium oxide, which has a non-porous ability, preventing corrosion. They slowly oxidize. With all the advantages of stainless steel that I have listed, they do have a major limitation, which is expense. They are very expensive because of the chromium and other alloy materials. If you don't mind the price or you want to invest in your water tanks, stainless steel material for the water tank is the best way to go.

FACTORS TO CONSIDER WHEN CHOOSING THE BEST WATER TANKS FOR YOU

Size For Your Needs

Now, after getting your preferred material choice for your water tanks, knowing the right size you need is the next step. Your various rainwater needs will determine how big or small you want your storage containers. These should be able to accommodate all your water needs conveniently.

Storage containers can give you access to large amounts of water whenever you need it. You can rest assured that with this quantity, you can satisfy your various needs like cooking and doing your laundry with absolute peace of mind. Getting the right size for your water storage tank depends on different factors that you need to observe and decide which is the best for you.

These factors include:

1. Knowing your needs

You need to know why you are getting a water storage tank. Is it for personal use like drinking or for complimentary use like a backup option for an existing water supply and your daily needs? If you are looking to create your own independent water source for all your potable and non-potable needs, look at your water bills over the last year to find out how much water you are currently using. On average, a family of four will use 176 gallons (660 liters) per day, which is 5,280 gallons (19,800 liters) per month. If that is the water usage you want to replace, a tank with at least 5,000 gallons (19,000 liters) capacity is best.

You may, on the other hand, be looking to start small and only use your harvested water for your backyard garden. In that case, many rainwater harvesting barrels available at hardware stores have a 50 gallon capacity. IBC totes have a wide range of capacities but are most commonly around 300 gallons. To estimate how much water you are currently using to water your garden, it's helpful to know that a standard garden hose delivers 17 gallons of water per minute. That means if you spend 15 minutes watering your garden, you are currently using about 255 gallons of water. In most places, it does not rain every day to refill your collection tanks for tomorrow's garden watering. This means you will likely use whatever is available in your tank at the time, as you probably won't have enough water stored to finish the job every day. Don't let this discourage you! Whatever amount you save from becoming stormwater runoff is still water conserved! Be proud of the difference you are making —every drop of water matters.

I always try to remind people that starting small is better than never starting at all. You can always connect one or more additional tanks later to expand your storage capacity after you have your rainwater harvesting system set up.

2. Rainfall in your location

It's normal in most environments to have dry spells where it won't rain for days, and you'll need to use the water you've saved. On other days, you will get a heavy rain that sufficiently waters your garden and fills your storage containers so much they overflow. You can never predict exactly what Mother Nature is going to do, and that's ok. If your goals for rainwater harvesting are to start small and begin to make a difference in water conservation, this is perfectly fine. Just go with whatever comes your way and enjoy the process as you learn and grow on your water harvesting journey.

If, however, you want to do the most possible with your harvested rainwater and you live in an area with very little rain or large gaps of time between rainfalls, getting a large water storage tank will be best for you. Since, for you, it's not days, but more likely weeks until your next rainfall, you don't want any overflow to escape from your storage container so that you have it available for the coming dry times. It's advisable for you to get the largest container you can with the amount of space and money you have available.

3. City rules

Some cities have rules for water storage tanks, and you may want to check your city rules for their water storage tank rules. I would recommend that you pick out water storage containers that are large enough to satisfy your neighborhood fire code conditions. Some countries like Nepal require their occupants far away from the fire station to have more than 3,000 gallons (about 12,000 liters) of water as a backup for a fire emergency.

4. Available space

Storage tanks can be small or very large, so they could require a lot of space. Before getting a storage tank, you should evaluate your available space. If needed, go for a small size that can accommodate your space or opt for an underground tank.

REASONS WHY YOU SHOULD CLEAN YOUR TANKS

There are several reasons why cleaning your tanks should be on your to-do list. Sediments in the water of storage tanks settle after some time, forming scum at the bottom of your tank. Light-colored or transparent tanks will encourage algae growth and contaminate the water. Getting a black water tank or painting your water tank black to prevent sun rays from actively passing through the tank is an excellent way to reduce and prevent algae growth.

Rusting reduces the physical properties of your storage tank, allowing other microorganisms entry. Water storage tanks made from steel especially have low corrosion resistance. The rust formed during this oxidation process affects and contaminates the water. Ingesting this contaminated water long-term can lead to sickness.

Cleaning your tanks regularly is an active way of caring for your family. Those substances that get leaked into the stored water are bad for the body, especially if you have a baby or little kids.

Methods for Disinfecting

1. Pre-Storage Treatment

Cleaning the tank isn't the only step you need to take to have a clean water supply from your storage tank. The pre-storage treatment is the treatment that you do to remove large debris from the rainfall going into the storage tank. Diversion and screening are two processes used in treating water before entering the storage water tank. When you divert, just as the name implies, you will be diverting the first bout of rain from the rainwater runoff. This has been found to have the largest particles and debris. This is accomplished by using a first flush diverter.

The other method of pre-storage treatment is screening. These are screens or net-like structures placed in the passage of the rain. Large debris still present in the flow of water is sieved off by using rain screens or gutter mesh. Keep in mind, the pre-storage treatment doesn't make the tank's water dirt-free because some tiny particles can pass through the screens, but it is a good first step in keeping your water tanks clean.

2. After-Storage Treatment

The after-storage treatment is done in the tank before use. The after-storage treatment involves two series of treatments: filtration and disinfection. The level of treatment given to stored water differs depending on where you got it from and how you will be using it—for personal use or irrigation. Whether your stored water is obtained from rainfall, underground, or surface reservoirs determines the level of treatment it will need. Water from underground sources needs little treatment compared to water gotten from rainfall or surface reservoirs.

I. Filtration

Cartridge filters are used to filter out pathogens, chemicals, algae, toxins, and microbes in the water supply. When the water supply is being used, it passes through various levels of filtration, filtering out the particle size by size depending on the cartridge size. Filtration is especially needed for water with a high level of sedimentation.

II. Disinfection

This is the last and final stage of the after-storage treatment. Some tiny microbes that are small enough to pass through the cartridge filters are killed in the disinfection stage. Disinfection of rainwater can be through chlorination, UV light, or ozonation.

a. Chlorination: This is the most common method to disinfect the water supply. Chlorine is added to the water in small quantities and kills any harmful microbes or pathogens that can harm you or your family. Chlorine has the advantage of disinfecting the distribution supply system as it passes through. In small amounts, chlorine is safe to consume in water, but it must be used in moderation and with caution.

There are different types of chlorine, for example, 4%, 12.5%, and 65% chlorine solution. The amount of chlorine added to water in your tank depends on which percentage of chlorine you get. The higher the percentage of chlorine, the less you will need to add. Be sure to carefully read the instructions on the kind of chlorine you purchase before using it. Chlorine can be toxic if too much is used.

Wherever you purchase chlorine should also sell chlorine test strips, so purchase those also so that you can test your water before drinking it. Up to 4 milligrams per liter is considered safe for consumption. Test your water 30 minutes after adding chlorine to make sure it has at least 0.5 mg/L, as that is an adequate amount to ensure the water has become safe. If it does not have that much chlorine at that time, add more and test again after another 30 minutes.

b. Ultraviolet light: UV light is another great method to consider when disinfecting. This kind of disinfection is mostly used in industries rather than for home use because of its cost and the dangers of UV light on the body. People who work close to UV light put on protective gear and goggles to reduce the intensity of the rays.

It is one of the most effective disinfecting methods, but only when the water is clear. In unclear water with particles, the UV rays can't see through, and many microbes and bacteria remain alive after the process. UV light can be added to the regular plumbing system in your house with a filtration system. The UV bulbs should be changed every 6 months.

c. Ozonation: When used in the correct quantities, ozone is a safe and effective way to purify air and water. It works more quickly than chlorine and does not leave behind any by-products in the water. Ozone is an inorganic gas that disinfects the water supply by oxidizing the microbes and bacteria in your water supply. You can purchase an ozone generator from rainwater harvesting supply stores and websites.

For any way you decide to filter and disinfect your water, it is wise to test the water before the first time you drink it. For a new system, it can take a few cycles of water going in and out of your conduits and storage container for water to come through your final filtration system completely clean. This is normal and nothing to worry about, but very important since you do not want yourself or your family to drink contaminated water. I also recommend testing your water at least every week for the first 2-3 months after installing a new system. If you are getting consistently safe results, you can switch to testing once every three months. You can find drinking water test strips online or at many hardware stores. They aren't very expensive, so it's worth it to make sure you don't give yourself something that could make you sick.

If you will only be using your stored rainwater for non-potable uses, you will only need to be concerned about going to these extents to purify water if you live in an area with heavy pollution or if your catchment area is especially dirty or contaminated. Again, it's best to be on the safe side and test the water before using it on your flower garden or lawn. It's difficult to find test strips specifically for non-potable rainwater harvesting, but I've found that test strips for ponds are great for this purpose.

8

MAINTAINING YOUR RAINWATER HARVESTING SYSTEM

One fact no one can deny about the rainwater harvesting system is that it has brought hope and solutions to numerous people in different parts of the world! Let's take a look at Hiware Bazaar village in Ahmednagar district in India. The Hiware Bazaar Village was highly populated but had little or no rainfall to sustain their food crops. Since 1972, when the village started experiencing water scarcity, many alternatives have been implemented, from the building of a dam which later leaked, to selling and drinking country liquor instead of water. During the early 1990s, they tried something new. They taught members of the community valuable principles of conservation and rainwater harvesting, along with putting into action a plan to make it all happen.

A ban was placed on tree felling, and villagers were put to work implementing the rain harvesting scheme. Trenches and embankments were dug, and village tanks and drains were built to conserve water. Gradually there was an increase in water output. As the amount of water available increased, the whole village began to see massive changes that built on each other. More water led to an increase in grass productivity, which benefited their livestock. This led to an increase in the cow's output and the sales of milk, new wells were built, and people were able to grow more crops. Rather than the famines from mere decades earlier, they were assured of drinking water, crops, and thriving livestock.

For maintenance, the village head put laws in place to regulate the type and amount of food crops grown by each house to allow for an equal distribution of water supply for the villagers. Now, in the village of Hiware Bazar, the food crops grown depend on inches of rain. For instance, if there are 12 inches (300 mm) of rain, the villagers are assured of drinking water and permitted to plant three full crops. Rainwater harvesting still seems like a holy grail for the villagers of Hiware Bazar to date.

NECESSARY MAINTENANCE FOR RAINWATER HARVESTING COMPONENTS

Below is a list of components of rainwater harvesting systems showing the overall maintenance of the components involved in the rainwater collecting system. We will be starting from the top to bottom; from the rooftop, gutters, first flush diverter, downspout, conveyances system, tank, and finally the water disinfectors.

1. Rooftop

This is the first line of action of the rainwater harvesting system. And should be maintained annually. The general condition of the rooftop should be examined, and necessary repairs should be made to the damages. If your house is near a lot of trees, the branches of the trees close to the roof should be moderately and properly trimmed to reduce the number of dry leaves on the rooftop.

2. Gutters

There should be general cleaning of all the accumulated debris and leaves from the fall season. The gutter where the water flows into the downspout should usually be taken care of before the rainy season starts. It should also be cleaned monthly when rainwater collection begins. The gutters should be covered by a gutter mesh or leaf guards if there is none before, or the existing one should be cleaned and accessed for tears.

3. First flush diverter

The first flush diverter catches the first batch of rainwater, which is the dirtiest and contains the particles washed away from the rooftop. The first flush diverter screen should be removed and cleaned and water made to pass through it to flush out any clogs.

You should see to it that after every rainfall, the diverter is emptied. If the rain is light, you may only need to empty every 2 or 3 rainfall intervals.

4. Downspouts

Downspouts are pipes that drain rainwater supply from the rooftop directly from the gutters into the conveyances system. One major problem of downspouts is the frequent recurring clogging. Downspouts can become blocked when debris or fallen leaves from the gutters are swept in by the rainwater. Downspouts aren't permanently attached to the rooftop, so they provide access for easy removal of clogs. The downspouts should be cleaned and checked thoroughly for leaks and clogs before the rainy seasons. During rainy seasons it should be checked monthly.

5. Conveyances system

After the occasional checks before spring startup, debris and clogs should be removed. Though not all conveyance systems can be checked, which is why there should be a rain screen between the downspout and conveyance system. The rain screen prevents the entry of particles from the down-spouts into the conveyances, and as an advantage, it is self-cleaning. The rain screen is built at an angle of 45 degrees, allowing the debris to slide off and the water to conveniently enter the conveyances. The rain screen should be checked after every rainfall.

6. Tank

The sediment level in the tank should be checked monthly, tanks don't need repairs often, and most tanks last for at least 10 years before they develop faults. Every six months to a year tanks should be cleaned and sanitized. If you plan to use this as your drinking water, I recommend every six months. After 10 years, repairs should be done on the tank. It can be repainted black to limit the amount of sunlight entering the tank; this is not necessary if the tank is already reinforced.

For any tank used for drinking purposes, a potable rainwater tank must possess a removable and easy-to-access leaf strainer between the inlet pipe and the water storage tank. The fittings around the leaf strainer should be unscrewed, and the contents of the leaf strainer disposed of and cleaned. It should be returned and screwed back tightly.

7. Water disinfectors

UV light and ozone injectors are two mechanical ways to disinfect your water source, so they will need routine maintenance. As the UV light gets dimmer, the effectiveness also reduces. So it is advisable to change it every 6 months. An ozone injector should also be inspected every 6 months to make sure it is working correctly and any filters on the ozone injector should be cleaned.

HOW TO KEEP YOUR WATER STORAGE TANK CLEAN

You should clean your storage tank at least once a year or more frequently, depending on your location and water use. If you live in an area with lots of sediments in your water, I would advise cleaning your storage tank more than once a year, preferably two or three times a year. If the water in your storage tank is used for drinking, it should also prompt you to wash more than once a year.

Water in storage tanks can become dirty in many ways, either from algae growth, rust from the tank, sediments, bacteria, or other solid materials from the passage of rainwater into the tank. When the water in your storage tanks becomes dirty, some signs will be visible to you. When you notice your water takes longer to settle, it appears cloudy in a clean glass cup, or you see some detached algae, these are signs for you to wash your storage tank. Keep notes on how long it takes for you to see these signs between cleanings so that you can start to predict when your container needs to be cleaned.

Only a few pieces of equipment are used in washing a storage tank: bleach, bucket, mop or brush, chlorine test strips, gallons of water, and vacuum if available. Note: you shouldn't enter the tank if you are not duly trained in this.

Step-by-Step Guide On How To Wash And Disinfect Your Tank

1. Wash

1. Mix your cleaning solution of a tablespoon of bleach to a gallon of hot water.
2. Wash all cleaning equipment you will use in your solution to sanitize them.
3. Set aside a few gallons of water which you will use to rinse the tank after it is cleaned. The rest of the water can be emptied from the tank.
4. Scrub the sides and built up sediments on the bottom of the tank. If you have a pressure washer, that will work best. If not, you can purchase a long-handled scrubbing brush. Scrubbing by hand will take more energy, but it will get the job done.

2. Rinse

1. Rinse the sides and bottom of your tank with the water you set aside earlier.
2. Drain all the dirty water away from your garden and septic system, and you can vacuum any remaining water if there is a vacuum available. If your tank is small enough, you may be able to tip the tank to help drain the remaining dirty water.
3. Fill up the tank and drain it all out to rinse away any remaining dirt and cleaning solution. You can do this once or twice.

3. Disinfect

1. Household bleach contains 5.25% chlorine. To disinfect or sterilize your tank, fill up your tank and use household bleach at a ratio of 1 cup of bleach to 60 gallons of water.
2. Let the water sit in the tank for 24 hours.
3. After disinfecting, drain away all the water in the tank by running the taps away from your garden or septic system. This water is not good for your edible plants and could kill the beneficial bacteria in your septic system. Rinse the sides and bottom of the tank until the water coming out of the spigot no longer smells like chlorine. Now you can harvest enough rainwater to refill the tank and test for high chlorine levels using the chlorine test strips. If the chlorine level is high, drain the water, rinse again thoroughly, and retest.
4. Once your chlorine test shows levels of less than 4 milligrams per liter, your water is clean and safe for use.

WINTER WEATHER CONSIDERATIONS

Winter is a period of extreme climate change. Pipes are the most affected part of the rainwater harvesting system and they undergo extreme changes due to this climate intensity. You must take extra measures during winter to prevent pipes and other components from freezing. Pipes can also burst open when frozen, causing extra expense and labor to repair the damage. This process of protecting and insulating the pipes and conveyances system during winter is called winterization. If your supply pipe is buried well below the frost line, you do not need to worry about winterizing that part of your system. You will only need to make sure pipes above the frost line are well insulated before the first freeze comes. Also, be mindful of your water pump at this time. If it is below the frost line as well, no need to worry. But if it is above ground, ice going into the pump while it's operating can damage it. Pumps should either not be used during extreme freezing temperatures, or other methods like aeration or a heat pump should be applied to make the water dispensable.

If your entire system is above ground and is used only for outdoor non-potable uses, you won't be using it in the freezing temperatures. You will want to follow the below steps to empty your system and prevent damage from bursting pipes in the cold weather.

A Step-by-Step Guide on How to Perform Winterization

For you to winterize your conveyance system, some activities you need to perform include;

- Empty all water in the tank and inspect the container for leaks.
- Disconnect any hoses.

- Inspect and check for water in pipes, any water inside should be drained with the valves kept open.
- Water shouldn't be allowed to flow into the tank anymore but to and out of the first flush diverter. Always check if the diverter is functioning and not clogged.
- The valve should be left open after the pump, and the expansion tank should be drained.

If you live in a region that does not experience extreme winter changes but are worried about your pipes bursting, you can leave your tap open slowly for 6-9 drops per minute. This makes the water in the pipes move slowly, also hindering it from freezing.

ROUTINE MAINTENANCE SCHEDULE

Proper maintenance is crucial to the longevity of your rainwater harvesting system. The rainwater harvesting system is indeed a way to conserve water for future use, reduce water costs, and increase accessibility of clean drinking water, but this doesn't make it maintenance-free. Maintaining your conveyance system should be important to you as lack of maintenance reduces the effectiveness of the pump system and filters, disrupting the main reason for installing these filters, which is to produce a clean water supply. Below are some factors you should keep in mind and strictly adhere to for proper maintenance of your rainwater harvesting system.

After every 1-3 rainfalls:

- Empty pre-storage filters
- Maintenance is important in rainwater harvesting systems, most especially in the pre-storage filters. The first flush diverter, gutter mesh, and rain screen should be cleaned, and debris and other materials in them should be emptied. A little mistake can lead to chains of unnecessary problems. The rain screen is the easiest of these to clean because they are placed at an angle of 45°, which makes most of the debris slide off the screens on its own. The first flush diverter is only slightly more difficult. It won't empty itself like the rain screen normally cleans itself, but it's not too difficult to open the bottom and drain it after a rain.

Every month:

- Remove blockages in gutters and downspouts
- Rooftop gutters and pipes should be cleaned regularly to prevent the blockage of water passage and anaerobic fermentation. Good maintenance of the gutters and pipes improves the quality and quantity of the rain supply obtained from it. Dry leaves release tannins into the water, which is

dangerous for ingestion and can cause discoloration of the water supply.

Every three months:

- Test your water
- If you are using your stored water only for non-potable uses, this won't be as much of a concern for you. The most significant potential threat to your health is when you are drinking the water. But if you plan to water edible plants with your system, you want to make sure you are not introducing toxins that will then be eaten by you.
- For those of you who plan to make your stored water potable, regularly using drinking water test strips will ensure your water won't make you or your family sick.

Every six months:

- Check your pumps and after-storage filters
- If you use the ultraviolet light method of disinfection, the UV bulb should be changed every six months or as often as stated by the manufacturer.
- For those using an ozone injector, wash out the injector's filter at this time.
- Check water pumps and their filters, preferably every six months, to ensure they are still working

perfectly and perform any necessary maintenance recommended by the manufacturer. This is also normally the time a water pump will be due for an oil change.

- Wash your tank - Every six months to a year the tank should be washed so that any sediments at the bottom of the tank can be removed. To avoid doing this during the hottest and coldest parts of the year, I recommend marking a day in your calendar every spring and fall to perform this job. This is also a good time to check your tank for any needed repairs; repair leaks if damaged, and disinfect stored water.

Every year:

- Inspect catchment area - Every year, your catchment area should be inspected, removing all the dry fallen leaves and debris. Often, the rain will wash off the debris that falls on your roof. This is why you usually won't have to take any action more frequently. However, after a strong storm, there may be larger branches on your roof that won't easily slide off in a normal rain, or if they did, they might damage or break things around your house. This is why it's good to check after any especially strong storms. The roof is out of our normal eyeline, so you normally wouldn't notice something stuck on the roof unless you make a conscious effort to look. If you have trees growing close to your house, this is a good time to check and make sure they are not touching your roof. If they are touching your roof, be sure to trim them back to prevent roof damage.

- In some areas, roofs are prone to algae growth. It's in your best interest to catch this growth early before it has spread too far because it is much easier to clean it off your roof when it's only a little.

After all that work you put in up front to install your system, you want to make sure you get to enjoy the benefits long-term. Committing to this routine maintenance will ensure a well-functioning rainwater harvesting system for years to come.

9

TROUBLESHOOTING AND SAFETY CONCERNS

I want to share another story about how it only takes a small number of determined people to make a big difference. For this story, come with me to Sabari Terrace, a four-story apartment complex in India. Fed up with their dirty and unkept cisterns, a handful of residents got together to clean them up and make them usable again. This caught the attention of community members, and through donations and community contributions, they were able to commission a rainwater harvesting system on their terrace in the year 2017.

A housekeeping supervisor was employed to clean the terraces every few days to prevent debris, particles, and unwanted organic materials from clogging the pipes. Because of the large amount of catchment area they were able to develop, they are now able to harvest about 5,300 gallons (20,000 liters) for every hour of rain.

Because of this, residents in the city are inspired by the rainwater harvesting success story of Sabari Terrace and are now trying to emulate the same model in order to defeat the water crisis situation that has plagued the city. The initiative and determination of a few people have spread to help an entire city.

HOW TO REMOVE STRANGE SMELLS FROM STORED WATER

Although smelly water can result from a variety of factors such as the storage tank, length of time the rainwater was stored, and so on, there is no need to panic even if your rainwater begins to smell. Even with a little smell, it's probably still fine for your plants. However, just like all stagnant water can be a breeding habitat for algae and insects, rainwater isn't safe for drinking. And while you can still water plants with it, it's advisable that when watering plants such as vegetables, you don't pour directly on the vegetables or foliage but pour the water around the base. In addition, you can also endeavor to rinse your vegetables with clean water before cooking or eating them.

Rotten egg-like odor

This is the smell of sulfur. Even if your water is treated, it can still smell, but mostly water with a sulfur odor has a high sulfate content and low chlorine residue. For example, if your tap water smells like sulfur, it may be that you are at the end of the city water supply distribution, so there is a substantial decrease in the chlorine residue. The smell comes because microorganisms increase in number due to the low quantity of chlorine in the water to disinfect them.

There are two possible causes for the water in your tank smelling bad:

1. Microorganisms binding to sulfur
2. No activities in the water supply

1. Microorganisms Binding to Sulfur

If the problem is from microorganisms as they react to sulfur and form high levels of hydrogen sulfide, 2 milligrams per liter of chlorine bleach should be added to the water tank. The chlorine disinfects the microorganisms, reduces their amount, and as a result, reduces the hydrogen sulfide, which causes the bad smell to eradicate. Let this set for 24 hours, and then check for the smell. If there is still a smell, test to see how much chlorine is in the water and then add more. According to the CDC, up to 4 milligrams per liter of chlorine is safe in drinking water. Continue to add chlorine, wait, and test until the smell is gone.

A water purifier that removes hydrogen sulfide can be installed in the tank to prevent the reoccurrence of this rotten egg smell. There is a high probability that it will occur again if the water in your location has a high level of natu-rally occurring bacteria.

2. No activities in the water supply

When the water stays inactive for days, it can give off the bad, rotten egg smell to show that the water in the tank is poorly aerated. You can aerate the tank yourself by hand very simply. Scoop out a pitcher of the water, hold it up high above the tank, and pour it back in. This will encourage the water to pick up oxygen and bring it down to the rest of the tank. This method is useful if you have a small tank and don't want to spend money on an aerator. With a small tank, it may be infrequent that water sits for days without any being used, so it is unlikely the tank will quickly get that smell again. If you have a large tank, the amount of time it would take to aerate the entire water supply by hand is prob-ably not feasible. In this case, you can purchase an aerator that fits the size of your water tank. After you place it in your tank, let it run for 2-3 hours and check for the smell. The size of your tank and air pump will determine how long it will take to remove the smell, but aeration generally elimi-nates the rotten egg smell faster than chlorine.

HOW TO DEAL WITH BLOCKAGES

Blocked pipes can lead to many other problems, from stag-nant water, which produces foul smells, to rusting of the plumbing materials, which also serve as breeding grounds for mosquitoes. It can also cause a backflow of water since the normal route is blocked, and the water may redirect to other places you don't want it to go. Below are various ways you can deal with blockages in your pipes;

Rooftop leaves

One major factor that blocks pipes or rooftop gutters is leaves. Therefore, start from the rooftop and remove all the fallen leaves or debris that has settled in the gutter, preventing the passage of water. If when you're outside your house, you can see leaves and debris sticking out of your gutter, that's a sign your gutter is blocked.

The leaves can be picked off, and the gutter will be free for water flow. To get ahead of that problem and keep those things from falling into your gutters, gutter mesh should be placed over the gutters.

Downspout

The downspout is the pipe joining the gutter to the conveyance system. If the gutters are clear, but water is still not flowing into your storage tank, it is due to a clogged downspout. Some leaves or debris may have gotten through the mesh between the downspout and the gutter and got stuck in the downspout. Debris usually gets stuck at the spot where the downspout bends. To be sure of the location of the clog, you can try tapping on the downspout; this tapping action will give a resonant sound, and when the sound becomes dull, that's where the debris is located.

The particles can be removed by manually pushing through from the gutter with a stick or water under high pressure. If this trick doesn't work, you may have to unscrew the downspout if you can and handpick the debris off. The downspout should be screwed back as tightly as possible.

Drainpipes

In some settings, the downspout is connected to the drain pipes, and this is the hardest clog to get through. The drainpipes may lead to a storage tank underground or any other storage equipment. It is always better for a downspout not to be connected to the drainpipes in such situations. The downspout should have 2 inches to 3 inches of space between it and the drain pipes. A rain screen should then be placed over the pipes to prevent any debris from the downspout entry into the pipes.

If drainpipes are clogged, pass water at high pressure to dislodge or use a plumbing snake to clear the clog.

If not taken care of quickly, the situation can get worse if the blockage is due to a plant growing in the pipe. At that point, if your drainpipe is above ground, you will need to dispose of it and install a new one. If the drainpipe leads to an underground tank, if you catch it early, you should be able to remove it with a plumbing snake. If this doesn't work, you'll have to get to digging to find and remove the problem.

STEPS TO TAKE WHEN YOUR WATER IS CLOUDY

Why is my water cloudy? How can I make my water clear? My water is not clear; is it contaminated? These are some of the most popular questions about cloudy water.

Cloudy water can be a major cause of concern, worrying if the water is safe to drink or not. Most of the time, cloudiness in your water will not affect your health it is completely fine for watering your garden. Cloudy water is most often a result of tiny air bubbles in the water. It may also be a result of other factors, but most times, it is due to these air bubbles.

To know if the reason your water is cloudy is because of air bubbles, carry out the following test. Fill a clear cup with water. Put down the cup for a couple of minutes. If when you come back to the water it is clear, the problem was air bubbles and you have nothing to worry about. If the water is still cloudy, it is because of other factors. Having particles in water reduces its quality; the cleaner the water is, the better it tastes.

Below are some of the common ways to correct cloudy water. They include:

1. Sediment Filter

Sediment filters are little devices fixed to your faucet. They contain activated carbon cartridges, which trap particles and sediments in your water supply. To be honest, all tap water has tiny pieces of particles in them, although in a very minute quantity. Particles and sediments in high quantity cause cloudiness in your water.

2. Thorough cleaning of the tank

Washing, filtering, and sanitizing the tank's water will greatly improve the water's quality and color. When the tank is overdue for a cleaning, it can cause the water to become cloudy. Check your tank to confirm if it's the cause of the cloudiness. If your tank is dirty, a good cleaning should fix your cloudy water problem.

3. Aeration

Though a less likely source of the problem, methane in your water can cause cloudiness. Methane in water is usually limited to regions where the water supply is near an oil rig or natural gas drill. Methane is a non-toxic gas but flammable, so you don't want to have it in your water supply. Methane in water can make it cloudy, but it is hard to detect because it has no smell. However, a quick check can be done to ensure methane isn't in your water; place a glass full of water and light a match a little bit over it. If methane is present in the water, it will flare up a bit.

When you are sure methane is in your water, you will need an aerator to correct the problem. The aerator allows the gas to escape into the atmosphere, leaving you with clean water.

WHAT CAUSES COLORED WATER

☐ Problem:

Mold and algae in water cause the water to be colored. Algae in water give it a greenish look, and mold makes the water black. This is most times a result of the dirty tank with sediments serving as habitats for the successful growth of mold and algae.

☐ Solution:

Just like the solution to most problems that can occur with your rainwater harvesting system, a thorough cleaning works wonders. If this becomes a recurring problem for you, consider cleaning your water tank more often.

☐ Problem:

When the protective zinc layer of the pipes is peeled off completely, the water comes in contact with the pipe's inner layer giving the water a brown color.

☐ **Solution:**

Unfortunately, if this is the cause of your water turning brown, you will need to install new pipes.

☑ **Problem:**

When the anode rod in your water heater is completely rusted, the hot water produced by the water heater turns brown.

☑ **Solution:**

First, check if this is the problem by checking the color of your cold water and your hot water. If they are both brown, the water heater is not your problem. If only the hot water is brown, you need a new anode rod.

SAFETY MEASURES TO FOLLOW DURING RAINWATER COLLECTION

1. Water Tank

The most important safety rule to follow during rainwater collection is to ensure your tank is always covered. Children are curious and tend to stumble into trouble they don't see coming. If your tank is large enough to fit a person, specifically a child, a safely locked cover will prevent someone from stumbling into your tank and getting trapped. Ensure your tank is not within the reach of children, and don't leave a ladder beside a tank. That is just inviting curious little ones to climb up and potentially hurt themselves.

Also, double-check to ensure the foundation that is holding your tank is hard and sturdy enough to carry the tank's weight. Tanks occasionally fall when their support is weak, this can cause flooding or falling on people if they are within reach.

2. Ladder safety

Maintenance of the rooftop gutters is one task that can't be avoided during rainwater harvesting. Falls from the roof or ladder are also common. Be sure your ladder is placed well on an even surface and sturdy before climbing. Concentrate while cleaning the gutters and avoid distractions.

3. Rainwater

Rainwater isn't always as pure as people believe. They can mix with chemicals that dissolve in the air before falling on the roof, where they then mix up with more microbes and particles. You should never drink them without filtering and disinfecting. Ingesting harmful chemicals is bad for your health, and you should be mindful of it.

4. Garden

Some people who use collected rainwater only for gardening and watering plants believe they don't need to go through all the processes of filtration and decontamination of the stored water. Untreated water can be used only for plants that aren't edible. Vegetables and other edible plants shouldn't be watered using unfiltered water. Your edible plants take up any chemicals in this water and end up in the body when consumed.

5. Stagnant water

You should watch out for stagnant water. When the collection system is blocked, this will cause stagnant water. You should ensure clogs are being monitored and cleared from the pipe immediately when you notice them to prevent stagnant water because it is a perfect housing area for mosquitoes.

6. Water Pumps

Install your water pumps with their electrical circuit to prevent interruption to the power supply. An external pump must be installed in a dry and well-ventilated location. When the water pumps are fixed, you should make sure they can easily be removed for any repair works. A device that switches on and off the pump when the water level is low or high should be installed alongside the water pumps.

7. Cleaning Agents

When disinfecting, use either hydrogen peroxide or chlorine. Never mix them both; it can produce a toxic gas that is dangerous to inhale. Check the instructions on the type of chlorine you purchase to ensure you don't use too much, as that can be harmful to your health.

8. Mosquitoes

I enjoy spending time outside, but the presence of mosquitoes can make it miserable. Here are a few things you can do to prevent your tanks from becoming a mosquito breeding ground:

- Fix a window screen material over any openings where mosquitoes could pass through and cover the barrel at all times.
- You can pour 1 to 2 cups (0.25-0.5 liters) of cooking oil on the surface if the water is to be used for purposes aside from drinking. This would prevent the larvae from getting into the water, trapping it at the surface level.
- Adding a mosquito dunk to the stored water; mosquito dunks kill any larvae in the water.
- Pour away the stored water if it is infected with larvae.

Safety precautions is never the fun part of rainwater harvesting, but it is important. Be sure to keep these things in mind with your system so that rainwater harvesting doesn't become a frustrating burden and you can keep enjoying the fruits of your labor.

CONCLUSION

All rainwater success stories I told in this book were started by creative people who were thirsty for a positive change in their communities. You can also make your unique success story by taking the bold step of creating your own rainwater harvesting system. The start of any project can look extremely intimidating, but this book can successfully guide you through the process of creating your own rainwater harvesting system and equip you with the right information on the proper maintenance of this system for years to come. By creating a rainwater harvesting system, you are taking full advantage of the wonderful gift of nature. It falls on your roof for free, and with some planning, you can use that free gift for outdoor needs such as watering your garden and livestock, irrigating fields, and household needs such as drinking, bathing, doing laundry, cooking meals, fire prevention, and flushing toilets.

Rainwater harvesting has been in existence for ages and has been practiced in many regions of the world, such as India, Mayan settlements, Rome, and the Middle East. Though the practice of rainwater harvesting began to decline, its numerous benefits (ability to save cost, conserve energy, and depend less on the general water supply) have successfully revamped the culture of rainwater harvesting.

There are two main reasons I love rainwater harvesting. First, by harvesting rainwater on any scale—large or small—you can make a real difference in the world. You read those success stories about people who took the leap of faith and started their projects. Some people had success quickly, while some were initially mocked. But in the end, they all positively influenced their community and the world. I mean, you heard their story even though you may be halfway across the globe. If more people like you start harnessing the power of rainwater harvesting, more people are going to take an interest in and be aware of this solution. And that's how even a small act can eventually lead to huge change. But this is not just something that helps other people; it helps you too. When we get down to the most basic things a person needs to survive, water is at the top of the list. Water is an absolute necessity. By harvesting rainwater, you don't have to rely on anyone else to provide something you need.

You can get it for yourself. If what you want is water independence, you can get it.

The other reason I love rainwater harvesting is that it's not a one-size-fits-all, cookie-cutter thing. I don't have to have the exact same system as someone else, and they don't have to do it the exact same way as me. You get to look at your own situation and do this the way you want. Do you want to start small with a rain barrel or two and use it to water your flowers and lawn? Go for it. Do you want to rent a backhoe and excavate a place for your cistern large enough to provide for all your potable and non-potable needs? Nice. You got this! Do you want to use a rain screen, gutter mesh, first flush diverter, water pump, and UV light filter? If that's what best fits your budget, available space, and water needs, then do it.

My aim in this book has not been to tell you one "best" way to do this. People may tell you there is one superior way, but in reality, one way does not fit everyone's needs. My aim in this book was not to tell you what to think but how to make your own informed decision. Each chapter in this book took you one step closer to deciding what will work best for you. From learning the components of a system to choosing tank size and materials to finding out how to maintain a successful system, this book has led you straight down the path towards achieving *your* goals. In chapter 6, I even described steps for creating different sizes of systems, so everyone knows how to get started regardless of what scale you want to begin.

No matter how difficult it may seem, let the success stories in this book and your personal water problems be your motivation. I wish you success on your rainwater harvesting journey. If you found this book helpful for you, **please take a minute to leave a review on Amazon.** More reviews help other people find the same useful information you did so that they can start their journey too. The miracle water village is a perfect example of how you can take advantage of your resources, no matter how little they are, to create a long-lasting solution to your water-related problems. So follow all the guidelines in this book and get to work. Happy harvesting!

Scan the QR code below for a quick review!